DARING FAITH FOR
SUCH A TIME AS THIS

Esther

KELLY MINTER

Lifeway Press®
Brentwood, Tennessee

Published by Lifeway Press® • © 2024 Kelly Minter

ISBN: 978-1-4300-8790-8

Item: 005846456

Dewey Decimal Classification: 222.9
Subject Headings: BIBLE. O.T. ESTHER \ FAITH \ GOD

To order additional copies of this resource, order online at www.lifeway.com; write Lifeway Resources Customer Service: 200 Powell Place, Suite 100, Brentwood, TN 37027-7707; fax order to 615.251.5933; or call toll-free 1.800.458.2772.

Printed in the United States of America

Lifeway Women Bible Studies

Lifeway Resources
200 Powell Place, Suite 100
Brentwood, TN 37027-7707

**EDITORIAL TEAM
LIFEWAY WOMEN
BIBLE STUDIES**

Becky Loyd
Director, Lifeway Women

Tina Boesch
Manager

Chelsea Waack
Production Leader

Laura Magness
Content Editor

Sarah Kilgore
Production Editor

Lauren Ervin
Art Director

Sarah Hobbs
Graphic Designer

Table *of* Contents

ABOUT THE AUTHOR

Kelly Minter is passionate about God's Word and believes it permeates all of life. The personal healing and steadfast hope she's found in the pages of Scripture fuel her passion to connect God's Word to our everyday lives. When she's not writing or teaching, you can find her tending her garden, taking a walk with friends, cooking for her nieces and nephews, riding a boat down the Amazon River, or walking through a Moldovan village with Justice & Mercy International. Kelly is also working on her M.A. in Biblical and Theological Studies at Denver Seminary.

A few of Kelly's past Bible studies and books include, *Ruth: Loss, Love, and Legacy*; *Encountering God: Cultivating Habits of Faith through the Spiritual Disciplines*; and *The Blessed Life*. To see a full list of Kelly's past studies and learn more, visit lifeway.com/kellyminter.

Kelly partners with Justice & Mercy International (JMI), an organization that cares for the vulnerable and forgotten with the love of Jesus in the Amazon and Moldova. Scan the code to find out more about JMI. And to learn more about Kelly's books, music, and speaking schedule, visit kellyminter.com.

Acknowledgments

I'm forever thankful for Beth Moore's Bible teaching in my life. She fanned the flame of my love for God and His Word in my early twenties, and she generously lent her support to me as a young author. She wrote a beloved Bible study on the book of Esther that has been cherished by women all over the world. I could not write my own study on this book of the Bible without gratefully acknowledging the path she has paved for so many of us Bible teachers and the impact she has had on my personal relationship with Jesus.

Dr. Craig Blomberg and Dr. Richard Hess from Denver Seminary were incredibly generous to me with their time and expertise on the book of Esther, not to mention all they have taught me across the Scriptures in my years at Denver. I am deeply grateful.

HOW TO USE THIS STUDY

Personal Study

Each week features five days of personal study that walk you through Esther. You'll find questions to help you understand and apply the text, plus insightful commentary to clarify your study.

Video Viewer Guides

At the end of each week, you'll find a page that provides space for you to take notes during the videos.

Bonus Content & Recipes

Included throughout the study are a few pages of extra reading to help broaden your understanding of Esther's culture and this story's place in biblical and world history. I've also included some of my favorite recipes for you to enjoy over the next seven sessions as you study Esther. I hope you enjoy!

Leader Guide

A free leader guide PDF is available for download at **lifeway.com/estherstudy**. The leader guide offers several tips and helps along with discussion guides for each session.

Study Questions

In each day of study, you'll find a mix of observation questions along with the following:

Personal Take questions invite you to record your thoughts on the meaning of the Scripture passage being studied.

Personal Reflection is a time to reflect on what you're learning—about God and yourself.

Personal Response questions challenge you to take action to apply or respond to what you're learning.

Introduction

SESSION ONE

For centuries, the book of Esther has been a favorite. It's enthralled us with its gripping story about a vulnerable, young Jewish girl turned queen of the Persian Empire. Esther, a literal beauty queen, possessed more than physical splendor. Her rich character and unflinching resolve, traits that developed over time, are an inspiration to us all. In many respects, Esther is the heroine we hope lives inside us. Hers is the against-all-odds, rags-to-riches story we cherish. Who doesn't want to know that our lives matter, that God has a purpose and a plan for us, even when—*especially when*—life doesn't look the way we thought it would?

For the Jews in Esther's day, the idea of life not looking the way they'd always imagined loomed overwhelmingly large. For starters, they were living in the Persian Empire, a nine-hundred-mile journey from their homeland of Judah. How were God's people supposed to worship without a temple or offer sacrifices without priests? How would they hear from God and be kept on the straight and narrow path of God's Word without the prophets? Would God be with them in this faraway pagan empire after their ancestors had turned their backs on Him? Were the scattered Jews in Persia *still* the people of God?

Perhaps you are asking similar questions today. We each have an ideal of what life is supposed to look like when following God. And when that image is marred by sickness, loss, betrayal, broken relationships, or our own selfish choices, we wonder if God can still use us. If He's still with us. If we're still His children.

For the longest time, I thought the book of Esther was primarily about Esther's heroic bravery on behalf of her people. And certainly, this is no small detail. But the book is about far more. It is ultimately a story about God and His covenant faithfulness to His people—no matter where they find themselves. It's a story that reminds us that nothing is too dark or complicated for God's redemption. It's a story that invites us to stand in our own time and day, boldly living for the glory of Jesus Christ.

I recently visited Corrie ten Boom's house in Haarlem, Holland. Corrie was an adult when Nazi Germany stormed into Holland and occupied her beloved country. Her father was a watchmaker whose family lived above their shop. There, they hid hundreds of Jews during the unfathomably dark time of World War II. It was a Dutch informant who eventually betrayed the Ten Boom family. While they saved hundreds of Jews as a result of their efforts, Corrie, her sister, and their father were sent to concentration camps. Only Corrie made it out alive.

As I ascended the narrow winding staircase to Corrie's bedroom, I could scarcely take in my surroundings. The floor boards creaked beneath my steps as though history itself were crying out. The original family Bible—the one from which the hiding Jews would read in short moments of respite—lay open to the Psalms on the dining room table. I stood on the upstairs balcony where some would escape for quick breaths of fresh air, praying not to be noticed by the Gestapo roaming the streets. I wondered, *Would I have risked my life in obedience to God's call, like Corrie and her family did? Like Esther and Mordecai did? Like the countless men and women who came before and after them?*

The book of Esther invites us to ponder these questions in our own day and age. Our time is not that of the Persian Empire or Nazi Germany. We live in our own time and place; yet, our call to follow Jesus is no less urgent. Yes, it will at times require daring faith, but a faith we don't have to find on our own. The book of Esther reveals that God is the One who resources the seemingly insignificant with astounding courage. Every time God calls His people He also equips them, and this has always been true. So, it remains true for you today. In the following weeks together, I pray you will hear the call of God on your life *for such a time as this.*

Watch the Session One Video

Use the space below to follow along with the outline points from Kelly's teaching. A leader guide is available for free download at **lifeway.com/estherstudy**.

1. Ezra and Nehemiah show God's activity in the lives of _____
_____. Esther
shows His activity in the lives of _____.

To access the video sessions, use the instructions in the back of your Bible study book.

Welcome
to the
Empire

SESSION TWO

The Esther Story

I love a verse-by-verse approach to Bible study, and I especially love it when we're making our way through Old Testament redemption stories. Each day of study builds anticipation, as if it were a suspenseful click up the ascending side of a roller coaster. I relish the moments when suddenly, somewhere near the end of a study, we discover an entire nation is spared from famine, a city wall is rebuilt, or a widowed foreigner becomes an ancestor of a world-famous king, and, boom, we're barreling down the tracks with our hair whipping in the wind. The slow and sometimes tedious verse-by-verse ascent proves worth it.

So, it may come as a surprise to you that for this study I want you to ride the roller coaster all in one sitting—in fact, on the very first day. Yes, today your assignment is to read the book of Esther in its entirety. Esther contains repeating themes that are more potent when taken in together. Plus, you will get more out of the rest of your study if you begin by knowing how the story ends. This will take approximately thirty minutes.

Also, if you happen to be thinking, *I've already read Esther once, or a zillion times, so I can just skip to tomorrow because I've basically already done the first day of Bible study without actually having done the first day of Bible study*—this doesn't count. God's ability to supply a fresh word for us is not limited by our familiarity with any given passage. May His Spirit speak richly to you today as you take in this remarkable book.

Read the following three reflection questions before you read Esther. Look for corresponding answers as you go. Get comfortable. Put away distractions. (I see you, social media apps.) Ask the Holy Spirit for freshly revealed truths. You can write your reflections at the very end, or write them as you go. Either way is fine. Just do it all in one sitting. If you're going through this study with others, plan to share your findings with your group. And if by yourself, your insights will serve you throughout our time together.

Personal Reflection:

What recurring themes do you see?

How is God both visible and invisible?

In one summary sentence, what do you think is the main point of the book?

READ OR LISTEN TO ESTHER 1–10.

Personal Response: After reading the story of Esther, what is your response to the Lord?

If you need a reference point, here is mine. *Lord, You are sovereign over all things, even pagan empires or the post-Christian culture I live in. I want to be a witness for the name of Christ in a way that naturally spills out of me. I don't want to waste my life hiding or being afraid of rejection or the negative things that could happen if I stand for You. Whether I'm in the palace like Esther, or in the courts like Mordecai, may I speak confidently the name of Jesus.*

I'm expectant for the next six weeks and look forward to tomorrow. Wonderful job today. I hope you enjoyed the ride.

Our Place in the Grand Story

When I attended my first Nashville Soccer Club game with my friend Bethany—a season-ticket holder—I had no idea what was going on. I detested soccer growing up, after getting nailed in the nose with the ball one too many times. "Pass me a ball I can legally catch with my hands" is my sports motto. Before Bethany and I reached the soccer stadium on our electric bikes (we are so urban), I had already asked her what our team's record is, how many games a year we play, how good we are compared to European and South American teams famous for their "football," and would soft pretzels be available? Once we took our seats, I asked for an explanation of the rules. I searched some of the players and discovered the goalie lives in my neighborhood. I now keep an eye out for him in the park, hoping he has a free T-shirt to give me. All that to say, the more context I had, the more meaningful I found the game. It's just plain boring, if not confusing, to walk into something cold.

If this is true of sports and events, let me assure you it is true of the Old Testament. Any time we enter an Old Testament story we are immediately separated by miles, millennia, and cultural milieu. And depending on what book we're opening, we may find ourselves anywhere from Eden to Egypt, Israel, Babylon, or Persia. Getting the bearings of where we are, who we're with, and, most importantly, what part of God's grand story we're in is a crucial step in our study experience.

Today we will gather some of these pieces to give us context for the events in Esther. This will help us know where Esther's story falls in the Story—the grand narrative of God's work from Genesis to Revelation. Not only will this process make studying Esther more meaningful, but we will also gain further insight into God's unwavering love for His people. For us.

Familiarize yourself with the biblical timeline on pages 18–19, then **READ GENESIS 12:1-3 AND GENESIS 17:3-7.**

God promised to make Abraham (previously Abram) into a great

_____(FILL IN THE BLANK).

Who would ultimately be blessed through Abraham (12:3)?

How did God secure this promise to Abraham (17:7)? Circle below.

A covenant   A contract   A legal document   The Ten Commandments

God promised Abraham three things in these passages: land, a countless multitude of descendants, and that all nations would be blessed through him. Write these below for future reference. This concept will be invaluable to our study of Esther.

God promised Abraham:

1.

2.

3.

After God made a covenant with Abraham, his family grew. The book of Genesis tells the story of the Patriarchs (Abraham's son, grandson, and so on) all the way through Joseph. During Joseph's generation, Abraham's descendants relocated to Egypt to escape famine in their dwelling place of Canaan.

Approximately four hundred years later, God's people had grown into a thriving nation within Egypt and came to be known as Israelites. The Egyptians persecuted the Israelites because of their increasing size, fearing they would overtake them in their own land. They subjected them to forced labor and killed their newborn sons. This is the story told in Exodus 1–15.

Circle this moment on your timeline, then READ EXODUS 2:23-25 AND EXODUS 3:1-12.

God called a man named Moses to lead the Israelites out of Egypt and into the wilderness, where they wandered for forty years before entering the promised land of Canaan, a turning point in their story. Once in Canaan, they were their own people living in their own land under the rule of their own God. Eventually, their contentment with this setup waned, and they demanded a king like the rest of the nations had. Israel hated to forgo the opportunity to be like everyone else—don't we all? This led to the disastrous crowning of King Saul, and after many years of turmoil, to the reign of King David. The Israelite monarchy was off to the races, and after several generations of this arrangement the results were mostly unimpressive. Still, God was faithful to His people. He made a promise to David during his reign known as the Davidic covenant.

> Find the Davidic covenant on your timeline and READ THE PASSAGE FROM 2 SAMUEL 7 noted there. Underneath it, write how long God promised David's throne would be established (v. 16).

> Now read over the remaining marks on the timeline to see what befell the nation of Israel in the years following David's reign.

In 587–586 BC Babylon's king, Nebuchadnezzar, attacked Jerusalem, destroyed its city and temple, and exiled the vast majority of the remaining Israelites to Babylon. But that wasn't the worst of it. God's glory left the temple and the city of Jerusalem as well (Ezek. 10–12). What did this mean for the covenant God made with Abraham all those years ago? What would happen to the land, descendants, and blessing for all nations when the one nation through which the blessing would come was decimated and scattered?

The book of Esther details the account of the Jews who lived in Persia *after the exile* (post-exilic age). It's a fascinating era of Israel's history because it straddles an in-between era of God's people. Life would never be the same as it was before the Babylonian exile, yet God's faithfulness would prove unwavering after it.

I want us to close today with a passage of Scripture that directly relates to the exiled remnant living in Babylon. This will also have ramifications for the people we'll soon meet in Esther.

> READ JEREMIAH 29:10-14.
>
> How many years would Israel remain in captivity? _____
>
> What was God's promise to His exiled people?

Jeremiah 29:11 may be familiar to you; perhaps you've heard it referenced in a message, seen it on a graduation card, or even memorized it at some point. It is well-known for a reason. In the depths of our being, we want to know that God has a plan for us; not just any plan, but one meant to prosper and not harm us, to give us a future and a hope. We want to know God listens to our prayers, and that He will be found when we seek Him, even if our selfish choices have carried us to Babylon or a city called "Broken."

Jeremiah's words were written to the exiles living in Babylon, those who lost their city, temple, priesthood, monarchy, and even their sense of identity. Through this prophet, God reminded His people that He would not forsake His covenant with them, even in the midst of such loss and devastation (Gen. 12). He would not break His promise to David about a throne that would be established forever (2 Sam. 7). Though all seemed hopeless, God was still authoring the story and would bring it to completion.

Jeremiah's prophecy was not written *to* us, but it is still written *for* us. Hold onto God's promises, my friend. No matter what you're going through, what you've done, or what has been done to you, God longs to bring you home to Himself. He is still writing this same story today.

Personal Response: What are you worried about at the start of this study? Do you question God's purpose for you? Are you concerned He doesn't "have a plan"? Take note of your concerns, while also declaring your trust in His goodness and His control over your life.

Personal Reflection: What have you learned in today's study about God's commitment to His people, even when they turn away from Him? How does this impact your life today?

Well done making your way through a brief look at Israel's history. Tomorrow we'll open our Bibles to the book of Esther. I can't wait.

Timeline

THE PATRIARCHS

Abraham
Isaac
Jacob
Joseph

GENESIS 12–50

THE EXODUS

EXODUS 1–15

2166*–1805 BC —— 2091 BC —— 1446 BC —— 1446–1406 BC ——

GOD'S COVENANT WITH ABRAHAM

GENESIS 12

THE WILDERNESS

EXODUS 16–40

SOLOMON BECOMES KING

1 KINGS 1

ASSYRIAN CONQUEST & CAPTIVITY

2 KINGS 15

—— 970 BC —— 931 BC —— 722 BC —— 587 BC ——

KINGDOM SPLITS IN TWO

1 KINGS 12–16

BABYLONIAN CONQUEST & CAPTIVITY

JEREMIAH 20–29

*Dates are approximate and based on
the timeline in the CSB Study Bible*

THE
PROMISED
LAND

JOSHUA 1–24

DAVID
BECOMES
KING

2 SAMUEL 5

1406–1380 BC — 1050 BC — 1003 BC — 1000 BC →

SAUL
ANOINTED
KING

1 SAMUEL 9–10

DAVIDIC
COVENANT

2 SAMUEL 7:8-17

BABYLON
FALLS TO
KING CYRUS'S
PERSIA

JOSHUA 1–24

ESTHER
CROWNED
QUEEN

ESTHER 2:17

539 BC — 486–465 BC — 479 BC

KING
AHASUERUS'S
REIGN

THE BOOK OF ESTHER

God's Sovereignty *Over* History

ESTHER 1:1-2

Occasionally, I make my twenty-something friends homemade dinners followed by Bible study and prayer. In return, they do their best to keep me relevant. You'll see some of their wisdom and insight show up throughout this study. During one of our Monday-night gatherings, my friend Carly shared that she is learning to take the Bible stories she was taught as a child and string them together across God's bigger story of redemption. She's studying the Bible not as standalone accounts, rather as chapters in a single story. This is exactly what I hope we'll accomplish as we study Esther. To do this, we have two more historical stops to make before jumping into the first two verses of Esther.

Yesterday, we learned that Nebuchadnezzar sacked Jerusalem and carried its people away into exile in Babylon in 586 BC. Even in exile, God gave a good, perhaps even surprising, command to His children.

READ JEREMIAH 29:4-7.

Personal Reflection: It would be easy to feel like all you could do is "decrease" in a time like this (v. 6). How does God's command to thrive in a pagan land encourage, challenge, or surprise you?

Decades passed and the exiles found jobs, built homes, and raised children in this foreign land. Then, in 539 BC (about fifty years after the Israelites had left Judah), the unthinkable happened.[1] The great Babylonian regime fell to King Cyrus and his Persian Empire. But something else followed that became one of the most important historical events in Israelite history.

READ EZRA 1:1-5.

In the first year of King Cyrus's reign, what did he allow the Jews to do? (After the exile, Israelites became known as Jews.)

Who stirred Cyrus's spirit to allow the Jews to return to Jerusalem and rebuild their temple (v. 1)?

Personal Take: What do these developments in Ezra's opening verses tell us about God's involvement and rule in our world today (also known as His sovereignty)?

Personal Reflection: You may have been, or may be now, at the mercy of someone who doesn't know or revere God. How does this passage encourage or strengthen you?

Perhaps you noticed the mention of the prophet Jeremiah in Ezra 1:1. King Cyrus's decree was the beginning of the fulfillment of Jeremiah's prophecy—the one we read at the end of yesterday's study (Jer. 29:10-14). God's work is not limited to believers. He is sovereign over all rulers, nations, and peoples. He will accomplish His purposes. No person, no matter how powerful or godless, can stop Him.

We're now ready to begin our work in Esther. (And all the people said, *finally!*) From Ezra, turn forward two books and **READ ESTHER 1:1-2.**

During whose reign did the events of Esther take place?
King _____.

Some of your translations will use the king's Persian name, *Ahasuerus*, and others will use his Greek name, *Xerxes*. They both refer to the same king. We will use Ahasuerus throughout our study.

View the timeline below.[2] How many years is Esther's coronation removed from Cyrus's decree allowing the Jews to return? _____

538 BC	536-516 BC		479 BC	457 BC
Cyrus	Darius		Ahasuerus	Artaxerxes
Allows Jews to return	Jewish temple rebuilt		Esther becomes queen	Sends Ezra to Jerusalem

We're centuries and landscapes removed from the Persian Empire, so the name King Ahasuerus might not mean much to us. But his reign was significant in both biblical and world history.

Over how many provinces did Ahasuerus rule? _____

The Persian Empire was the world's largest superpower up to that point, as reflected in the map on the following page.[3] Circle King Ahasuerus's territory on the map.

Put a star beside the city of his throne on the map.

An approximately nine hundred mile journey separated Susa from Jerusalem.[4] Write that number in the space provided on the map.

—— Perimeter boundary of the Persian Empire
—— Persian Royal Road
  Heartland of Persia (Cyrus ascended throne)
  Territories gained by Cyrus (550 BC)
  Territories gained by Cyrus (547 BC)
  Territories gained by Cyrus (539 BC)
  Territories gained by Cambyses II
  Territories temporarily gained by Xerxes I

Wrapping our minds around these locations, distances, empires, and kings gives us an appreciation for how unlikely the survival of God's people was in the post-exilic period. The story of Esther began around 486 BC, when Ahasuerus came into power.

At this point in history, the ten Northern Tribes of Israel had already been scattered for more than two hundred years (since 722 BC).[5] And for approximately 100 years, the Southern Kingdom of Judah had been digging roots in Babylon (587 BC).[6] While a small segment returned to Jerusalem from Babylon under Cyrus in 539 BC, the vast majority stayed. *It is this vast majority of exiles who will be our focus in Esther!*

Thanks to a few books in the Old Testament, we're given perspective on both sides of the post-exilic Jewish experience. The books of Ezra and Nehemiah tell the story of God's activity in the lives of the exiles who returned to Jerusalem. The book of Esther tells the story of His activity in the lives of those who stayed. We can imagine the challenges that both groups of people faced.

For the returning Jews—those whose spirits God had stirred (Ezra 1:5)—the road back was a treacherous four-month journey. And when they arrived, it wasn't to the Jerusalem they remembered. Its former glory was long gone. The landscape lay battered. Perhaps more challenging, the people themselves needed renewal and restoration. The work ahead was exciting, but nothing would be easy.

The Jews who remained scattered across the Persian empire faced a different kind of challenge. They didn't have to uproot their families or risk their lives on a long journey. For the most part, the Persian empire treated its foreigners respectably. But Susa, the capital city of Persia, was miles from the land God had promised Israel. Without a temple, the Israelites couldn't worship the way they used to. They had to assimilate into a culture nothing like the one God had cultivated amongst His people.

The Jews who stayed where they were didn't have to ask the question, *How will we rebuild Jerusalem?* Instead, they were faced with a different one: *In this foreign land, can God rebuild us?*

> Based on the map alone, what's one possible reason so many of the Jews might have decided to stay where they were instead of returning to Jerusalem?

> Personal Response: If you lived during this time period and were given the opportunity to return to the battered city of Jerusalem to help rebuild the temple, bring spiritual reform, or rebuild the walls of Jerusalem, do you think you would have gone? Or would you have stayed in the foreign but now more familiar setting of Persia, living as a Jew in exile? (Keep Jer. 29:4-7 in mind.) Journal your thoughts.

The exiles who returned to Israel had to deal with enemies who opposed their rebuilding the temple and city walls, but at least they held in their hands hammers for God's house and scrolls carrying divine instructions dating back to Moses. For the Jews scattered in Persia with no temple, home city, or religious sacrifices, life had its own question—is God still with us?

> **Personal Response:** In what ways do you relate to the struggle of the exiles in Persia? In what areas of your life does God seem distant or absent?

Pastor and theologian Iain Duguid masterfully gets at the exiles' predicament. "They couldn't see this God, they hadn't heard from him lately, and in any case, they were living miles from the land he called his own. Did this invisible God still have what it takes—in terms of power and interest—to reach out and touch their lives?"[7] This is the question we can reasonably surmise the exiles in Persia lived with. And it's a question we must ask ourselves today. *Is God at work in our day and age, in the country we live in, under the government we find ourselves subject to, in the neighborhood that doesn't see life the way we do? Is He at work in our post-Christian culture?*

My prayer is that when we reach the end of our study you will see the hand of God more clearly in whatever place you find yourself, even when He is seemingly invisible.

A Display of Decadence

ESTHER 1:1-8

It seems that with every passing year our world becomes more and more divided politically, religiously, and socioeconomically. I can remember my grandparents saying similar things, so maybe this is nothing new, but it feels more severe. As believers, we pray for and faithfully pursue God's kingdom here on earth. But even when a country loses its way, when kings and presidents govern unjustly, and nations rise up against one another, we are reminded that it is God's Son, Jesus, to whom every nation belongs (Ps. 2). He, alone, is Lord (1 Cor. 12:3).

The Persian empire was home to countless worldviews because it was home to many ethnicities and religions. Throughout our study we will discover that, although the dispersed Jews in Persia were a world away from God's appointed land for them and lived under the rule of a pagan king, God was still at work and fully in control.

Esther's story opens with elaborate details about King Ahasuerus's empire.

READ ESTHER 1:1-8.

How long did the tribute to King Ahasuerus's kingdom last (v. 4)?

_____.

Who did the king invite to the banquet during the final week of celebration (vv. 3,5)?

Describe the vessels the drinks were served in.

The guest list for the king's feast was made up of the king's entourage, officials, and special guests.[8] Everyone, from the "greatest to the least." It was an enormous crowd by any standard. The opulent display was meant to inspire loyalty to the king, and according to history, to rally enthusiasm for a forthcoming military campaign against Greece.[9] The king likely wanted to assure his kingdom that Persia was the team they wanted to be on.

Personal Take:

What does verse 4 relay about the king's character? Make as many reasonable assumptions as you can.

What might it have been like to serve under the rule of a king like this? Detail both positive and negative aspects you can imagine.

Look back at verses 6-8. What stones, precious metals, fabrics, and colors are mentioned?

Personal Take: Why do you think the author included these elaborate details about the palace? Why are they important to the story?

FILL IN THE BLANKS: The king served wine so liberally that there were no _____, and every person was served whatever he or she _____ (v. 8).

Personal Take: What do the opening eight verses tell you about the Persian Empire of that time? (Go beyond responses like, *it was powerful and wealthy.*)

Beautiful settings delight me endlessly—a well-appointed piece of art, a nicely placed fern, a polished nickel fixture. I can think of nothing more enjoyable than when a thoughtful setting is home to a slow and elaborate feast. But when an inviting space turns into a display of materialism and pride, when feasts become avenues of drunkenness and decadence, and lavish gifts are used to buy the allegiance of others (as seems to be happening here), I'm reminded that God's good gifts can suddenly turn into deadly idolatry. This is the scene on which the curtains of the Persian Empire open.

Esther 1:4 reads, "He displayed the glorious wealth of *his* kingdom and the magnificent splendor of *his* greatness" (emphasis mine). The possessive pronoun *his* is the most significant word in the verse. For King Ahasuerus, everything was about him and his splendor.

READ THE FOLLOWING PASSAGES and <u>underline</u> what each verse says about pride.

To fear the Lord is to hate evil. I hate arrogant pride, evil conduct, and perverse speech.

PROVERBS 8:13

You adulterous people! Don't you know that friendship with the world is hostility toward God? So whoever wants to be the friend of the world becomes the enemy of God. Or do you think it's without reason that the Scripture says: The spirit he made to dwell in us envies intensely?

JAMES 4:4-8

In the same way, you who are younger, be subject to the elders. All of you clothe yourselves with humility toward one another, because

"God resists the proud but gives grace to the humble."

Humble yourselves, therefore, under the mighty hand of God, so that he may exalt you at the proper time, casting all your cares on him, because he cares about you.

1 PETER 5:5-7

Though King Ahasuerus's display of wealth was absurdly over-the-top, we can be equally guilty of highlighting our possessions and accomplishments in subtler ways.

Personal Response: Write a prayer in the space below, confessing any areas of pride. Think of even the subtle areas of self-promotion or selfish attention-seeking. God promises grace to the humble (1 Pet. 5:7).

As we study the book of Esther, we will make a habit of returning to Israel's history for continuity and understanding of God's covenant with His people. We will also regularly look forward to the New Testament. I'm calling the latter "Gospel Moments," where we will bridge truths and concepts found in Esther with New Testament counterparts.

GOSPEL MOMENT

Approximately four hundred years removed from King Ahasuerus's sprawling banquet where the mostly well-to-do sipped wine without restriction, Jesus gathered the sick, broken, and beaten down on a Galilean hillside. There, He announced the arrival of His kingdom. One can hardly imagine a kingdom more unlike the one that hosted elaborate feasts in Persia.

SLOWLY READ MATTHEW 5:2-10. Describe some of the differences between those feasting in Susa and those for whom the kingdom of heaven had come.

IN SUSA	IN THE KINGDOM OF HEAVEN

Even the most powerful empires crumble. Kingdoms come and go. Wealth eventually corrodes, and gluttony never satiates. History tells us that only four years after Ahasuerus's magnificent display of power and wealth, he suffered a significant defeat at the hands of the Grecian army. The humiliating loss cost him a great deal of his royal fortune. Esther's original audience would have recognized this irony at the opening of Esther's story.[10] The powerful king Ahasuerus was about to have a very great fall.

Though the Apostle Paul had a different kind of eating and drinking in mind when he penned Romans 14:17, his words are especially appropriate to today's study. "For the kingdom of God is not eating and drinking, but righteousness, peace, and joy in the Holy Spirit."

Personal Response: What is one action you can take today to pursue righteousness, peace, or joy *in the Lord*? Decide on an action you can commit to and take that step today.

Power, Pleasure, *and* Folly

ESTHER 1:9-12

In the movie *Saving Mr. Banks*, a film about the British author who wrote *Mary Poppins*, the illustrious Walt Disney tries to persuade P. L. Travers to sell him the rights to her book. Much of the movie spans the hardships of her life, casting her as a wounded and hardened creative, though not without a heart. Reluctant to sell out to Disney, she begrudgingly agrees to listen to the musical numbers composed for the potential film. While the Sherman brothers play their piano and belt out "Let's Go Fly A Kite," the scene cuts to Ms. Travers's 1950s high heel involuntarily tapping the floor to the enchanting tune. She can't help it. The fleeting scene of her tapping foot, without a word spoken or overt gesture made, serves as the hinge upon which the entire movie swings open. It was swift and subtle and remarkably powerful. No one needed to spell out the scene for us. We knew what was happening. Travers's heart was softening, and Mary Poppins was about to become a household name.

As we study the book of Esther, we will need to watch for tapping toes. Quick frames, with meaningful but subtle detail, will be priceless. Esther's literary genre is considered historical narrative by conservative scholars. Part of what this means is that the author doesn't give his opinion about the characters' actions; rather, he allows us to interpret those actions based on the unfolding story. He *describes* what happens rather than *prescribing* what we should do or how we should feel as a result.

As Christ followers who hold to the authority of Scripture and believe in its power to make us wise unto salvation (2 Tim. 3:15), we will do our best to interpret the people, behavior, and decisions in the book of Esther with help from the rest of the Bible. But we will also be watchful *within* the book of Esther for the subtle details the author includes, as well as the literary tools he uses that naturally draw us to certain conclusions.

WITH THIS IN MIND, READ ESTHER 1:9-12.

Who is introduced in verse 9?

On what day of the banquet did the king send for Queen Vashti, and what was his state of mind (v. 10)?

Why did the king want Queen Vashti to come before his banqueting guests and officials (v. 11)?

What was the king's response when Vashti refused his command?

On the final day of Ahasuerus's banquet, which was supposed to be the climax of his glory, the queen refused his request. This is not insignificant. "The beautiful Vashti, wearing her royal diadem, was a living trophy of his power and glory."[11] How was the king to show ultimate authority over his kingdom if he couldn't even garner respect in his own house? And how was he to inspire a military under his command if his own wife wouldn't come at his bidding? Vashti's courageous refusal was a massive blow to the king. He may have ruled 127 provinces, but it seems clear he had no idea how to love the one person who should have mattered most—his wife.

What negative behaviors and traits have you already learned about Ahasuerus? Detail as many as you can find in the text.

In Proverbs, we read, "A person who does not control his temper is like a city whose wall is broken down" (Prov. 25:28). What do you think this means?

Personal Take: What is your opinion of Vashti's refusal to go before the king? How do the traits you've listed about Ahasuerus inform your opinion?

NOW READ ESTHER 1:13-22.

With whom did the king confer to determine his next steps?

Personal Take: What was the advisor Memucan's main concern (vv. 17-18), and do you think it was a reasonable one? Why or why not?

What did the irrevocable decree mean for Queen Vashti (v. 19)? And what did Memucan hope it would mean for all the wives in Persia (v. 20)?

While the author hasn't come right out and said that the Persian Empire is a dumpster fire and its king a megalomaniac, he is giving us reason to feel deep skepticism about the Persian imperial regime.[12] For starters, king Ahasuerus is hot-tempered, drinks excessively, and views his wife as a pawn for his personal pride and the pleasure of his male guests. Some ancient rabbis and modern scholars suggest the king requested Vashti to appear naked, wearing only her crown. We can only imagine the courage it took for her to stand up to the king's exploitation, knowing it would most likely cost her the crown.[13]

When spurned by Vashti, Ahasuerus consulted his "wise men," who turn out to be anything but. Memucan and his six friends viewed Vashti's spurning of the king as a window of opportunity to seize control over their own wives. Instead of Ahasuerus taking time to heed wise counsel, his knee-jerk reaction publicized the very thing he wanted to conceal—Vashti's rejection of him. And in his angry haste he gave away his authority to cowards who thought that honor could be demanded (v. 20) and that being sexually exploited was synonymous with worthiness (v. 19).

Personal Reflection: It's tempting to write off this recklessly oppressive behavior as stuff of an ancient empire in a faraway land. But how do you see these same behaviors, values, or belief systems operating today in our own culture? (As you think of examples, also think about avenues of Christlike restoration. Otherwise, we can easily get stuck in unhelpful, judgmental thinking).

There are many places we can go in the New Testament to find truths that fly in the face of Ahasuerus's abusive treatment of Vashti and his counselors' fear tactics toward Persian wives. Perhaps none as clearly as in Ephesians.

READ EPHESIANS 5:1-3,21-25. Contrast these verses with the scene in Persia.

We see no hint of any of these Christian virtues in Ahasuerus, nor should we. He is as pagan as they come. And while the book of Ephesians brings helpful truths as we process Ahasuerus and Vashti's relationship as a married couple, Esther's author does not present the couple as husband and wife, rather as king and queen.[14] The big picture here is not solely about the horrors of oppressive marriages, or sexual abuse, or foolish counselors, or hot tempers, or alcoholism, or unchecked power, or greed, or hasty decisions—it's about *all of it*. It's about what life looks like when we're living under the empire of this world instead of in the kingdom of heaven.

Duguid insightfully writes, "The Book of Esther repeatedly invites us to compare and contrast the kingdom of God and the empire of Ahasuerus."[15] This is how we will end our week. By leaving Ahasuerus's hysterical and unstable empire for a moment and moving toward the kingdom of heaven.

For even the Son of Man did not come to be served, but to serve, and to give his life as a ransom for many.

MARK 10:45

GOSPEL MOMENT

How did Jesus's mission differ from Ahasuerus's in Esther 1:4?

What does this teach you about living for the kingdom of heaven versus the empire of money, power, and fame?

Why is it that, all these years later, sex still sells, beauty is a billion-dollar industry, and governments still oppress the powerless? You'd think a couple millennium would be long enough for us to have learned by now. The problem, it appears, is that we don't want to learn. We resist the One who will free us from the bondage of this misery, the One who gives righteousness, peace, and joy. Life and satisfaction are not found in the Ahasueruses of this world, nor in their clumsy advisors. They are not found in another drink from a grandiose goblet. If you are weary of living for the world's treasures, come to the One who offers rest for your soul, who leads you alongside still waters, and whose very life is the Bread that nourishes.

Personal Prayer: Spend some time thanking Jesus that He did not come in the spirit of Ahasuerus, but came to be a servant, One who would give His life for you.

Great work digging into the context surrounding the book of Esther. You covered a lot of ground this week and I'm so proud of you. I want to leave you with one final thought: No matter how far flung into exile you feel, no matter how many miles you've drifted from home, God's Word holds firm: "From there the LORD your God will gather you and bring you back" (Deut. 30:4, NIV). You need only turn to Him.

Lamb Vindaloo

This is a wonderful dish anytime, but especially in the fall and winter when you're wanting something warm and cozy. It's nice to throw in lamb on occasion in a world of chicken and beef, and the flavors are a nice change-up from what most of us are used to. While this dish may look complicated at first, it's really just throwing several ingredients into the food processor to make a paste, and the rest is breezy.

INGREDIENTS FOR LAMB

- 1 ½ pound lamb, pre-cut into approx. 2 in. pieces
- 2 Tbs ghee (or unsalted butter)
- 1 large white or yellow onion, thinly sliced
- ¾ pound new potatoes or round potatoes
- 2 cups chicken stock
- 1 15 oz. can crushed tomatoes
- Fresh cilantro for garnish

INGREDIENTS FOR PASTE

- 2-4 dried chiles de árbol, depending on desired heat
- ¼ cup distilled white vinegar, plus 2 Tbs for later
- ½ onion
- 3 garlic cloves
- 1 ½ in. fresh ginger, peeled
- 2 tsp cumin
- 2 tsp garam masala
- 1 tsp ground mustard
- 1 tsp turmeric powder
- ½ tsp ground clove
- 1 tsp kosher salt
- 1 tsp sugar

DIRECTIONS

PASTE: Soak the dried chiles in ¼ cup hot water and ¼ cup white vinegar until soft (about 20-30 minutes). Once soaked, in food processor puree peppers, 2 Tbs of white vinegar, onion, garlic, ginger, all spices, sugar, and salt. Taste the paste for heat. Add more chiles, if desired.

FOR DISH: Toss lamb in half the paste until evenly coated. Cover and marinate in the fridge for at least 4 hours. Cover the remaining paste and store in fridge. Melt the ghee (or butter) in large sauce pan. Add thinly sliced onions and caramelize about 20 minutes. Add remaining paste and stir to coat onions. Add lamb and all marinade juices and cook until browned. Add potatoes and stir to combine. Add chicken stock and crushed tomatoes. Bring to a simmer and cook until lamb is tender and potatoes soft, around 40 minutes. Serve over saffron rice with naan bread. Garnish with cilantro and an (optional) dollop of Greek yogurt.[16]

Watch the Session Two Video

Use the space below to follow along with the outline points from Kelly's teaching. A leader guide is available for free download at **lifeway.com/estherstudy**.

1. The spirit of empire is about having _____

_____, _____,

_____.

2. The spirit of empire is not about _____;

it's about _____.

3. Though the book of Esther never mentions _____,

it makes us _____.

4. Jesus doesn't promise _____;

He promises _____.

To access the video sessions, use the instructions in the back of your Bible study book.

God's People
in Faraway Places

Meet Mordecai *and* Esther

ESTHER 2:1-7

There are many things I hope this study will accomplish in your life. One of them is the awareness that God desires to use you in whatever place or season you find yourself. When the consequences of sin infiltrate our families or closest relationships, we can start to believe the lie that God no longer has a place for us. When He's silent, or we're isolated from other believers, or our job is as secular as secular can be, we wonder if we're living Plan B of the Christian life. If the book of Esther teaches us anything, it's that God works through His people, sometimes in the most unexpected places and situations.

As we begin chapter 2, nothing will prove more surprising than Esther and Mordecai stepping into the storyline and changing its trajectory. First, because they are lowly outsiders without their own place or prominence in the Persian Empire. But second, and perhaps more surprising, because nine hundred miles removed from Jerusalem—and her temple, prophets, and priests—God is still at work in His people.

READ ESTHER 2:1-4.

Personal Take: Based on verse 1, do you think Ahasuerus regretted his decision to remove Vashti? Why or why not?

We're not expressly told how the king felt about his decision to depose Vashti. But we are told that after time had passed, and he'd cooled down from his rage, he was mulling it over. The Hebrew word for *remembered* in verse 1 carries overtones of regret, or at the very least gives the impression the king is wondering if he made the right decision. Personally, I think the king may have wished he hadn't acted so hastily.

This may remind you of a time when you made a rash decision out of hurt or anger, or in the middle of foolish behavior—a decision you couldn't undo, like Ahasuerus's irrevocable decree.

Personal Response: What is one way you can guard against making important or lasting decisions when emotions are bubbling over?

According to verse 2, who devised the extensive plan to find a new queen for the king (circle below)?

The king himself   A prophet   The king's advisors   The religious leaders

This was not the first time the king's advisors suggested a plan and then carried it out themselves (Esth. 1:16-22). What does this pattern tell you about the strength, or lack thereof, of the king?

A new character named Hegai is mentioned. What was his role in relation to the king?

The ancient historian Herodotus records that Persian kings chose their wives from seven noble Persian families.[1] It appears Ahasuerus's desperation caused him to break from this tradition, instead collecting beautiful virgins from across the empire and entering them into a beauty and bedroom-performance competition. The proposed plan is horrifying and was a terrible reality for young, beautiful virgins under Ahasuerus's reign. What is not as often recognized is that eunuchs like Hegai had it just as bad. Herodotus reports that every year, five hundred young men were taken from Assyria and Babylonia, castrated, and consigned to a life of service in the Persian court.[2] "Everyone's sexuality, and not only women's, was at the king's disposal."[3]

Personal Take: Based on verses 3-4, do you think the women taken into the harem were terrified by their plight? Or do you think they reveled in the opportunity to possibly be crowned the next queen of the Persian Empire?

It's tempting to paint a tamer, more placid picture of the environment in which the account of Esther is set. Many parts of the story would be easier to reconcile if we could sanitize these details. But it is precisely within the horror of a godless empire that God's people often find themselves. This is a tragic scene we must allow ourselves to sit in.

READ ESTHER 2:5-7.

The first main character to be introduced is _____.

What tribe is he from?

Judah   Asher   Reuben   Benjamin

How did he get to Persia?

The second main character is introduced with two names:
_____ and _____.

What is her relationship to Mordecai?

Cousin   Niece   Sister   Mother

What details are given about her in verse 7?

Verses 5-7 serve as a biographical interjection introducing Mordecai and Esther (notice how verse 8 picks up from verse 4). Up to this point, the lavish festivities of the Persian Empire have enveloped us, while the swells and crashes of the king's splendor and debauchery have rendered us unsteady. We've witnessed both his generosity and his greed, along with his irresponsible relinquishing of power to manipulative advisors. The last thing we expect the story to do is turn in the direction of two Jewish exiles.

But this is God's story, not Ahasuerus's. We're about to see that when God's people find themselves in ungodly places, nearly a thousand miles from home, they are not out of

His grasp. Mordecai's brief genealogy and his relationship to Esther set up the rest of the story.

TURN BACK TO 1 SAMUEL AND READ VERSES 9:1-2; AND 10:1,17-24.

Kish fathered a son named _____. Kish's son was from the tribe of Benjamin, and Samuel anointed him as Israel's first _____.

Mordecai wasn't just any Jew; he was a descendant of King Saul, Israel's first king. Israel's monarchy lasted a few hundred years—until King Nebuchadnezzar decimated Jerusalem in 586-587 BC, which we briefly addressed last week (p. 16). The biblical account of that important landmark is significant to our story in Esther. Let's read about it in 2 Kings.

READ 2 KINGS 24:1-4,8-17.

Personal Take: What stands out to you about the devastation?

Nothing was ever the same for Israel after the exile. Some Israelites returned to rebuild their decimated land decades later, while most remained scattered abroad as Jews. But life never went back to the way things were.

Personal Reflection: Do you have a "before and after" in your life, for good or bad? A time when you can look back and say, *At that moment, everything changed?* In what ways can you see God's faithfulness on this side of that event?

Those who remained in Persia's sprawling empire (the Jews in Esther) did so without their temple, priests, or sacrificial system, though there is evidence to suggest that the handing down of biblical texts persisted.[4] With each successive generation, presumably more and more customs were lost, and more and more assimilation into Persia's culture became a reality.

Tumultuous times can thrust unusual opportunities upon us if we have the eyes to see them and willingness to accept them. We're not told how Esther's parents died, but we know she was an orphan in a foreign land, even though she'd been born into that land. One of the facts of the story that's often overlooked is that Esther was not only a Jew, a foreigner, and an orphan—she was also adopted by Mordecai (2:7). Mordecai's adoption of Esther is biblically symbolic of God's relationship with His people, Israel (Jer. 3:19).[5] It's one of the book's more subtle but significant reversals—the Lord sets the lonely in families (Ps. 68:6).

> How does Mordecai's adoption of Esther contrast Ahasuerus's summoning of virgins?

We'll study the significance of Mordecai and Esther's names tomorrow. But for now, I want the power and surprise of verses 5-7 to impact you the way it did the original reader. No one was expecting a Jewish man and his adopted daughter to play such a significant role in Israel's story. While God is never mentioned in the book of Esther, Mordecai's lineage is a direct reminder of God's relationship to His people and His promises to them. Would those promises still hold for a people who had resolutely turned their back on the Lord, been exiled into Babylonia, and remained in Persia, even after some may have had the opportunity to go home? This is one of the most important questions the book of Esther seeks to answer, and one we still ask in our own forms today: *Can God forgive me for my past sin? Can I still be used for His purposes, or have I lost my chance? Are the wounds left from abuse and abandonment too much for the Great Physician? Does the cross of Christ still apply to me?*

READ ROMANS 8:1-4.

GOSPEL MOMENT

How does Christ's accomplishment on your behalf minister to you (especially if you feel like you're in a distant place)?

Christ has set you free to live the life for which He created you. If God was faithful to His covenant promise to keep and hold the Jews after the exile, how much more will He hold you as His own after the cross of Christ.

UNDERSTANDING *the* DIFFERENCE BETWEEN *the* EXILE *and the* DIASPORA

When studying the latter parts of the Old Testament, it's helpful to understand the difference between the exile and the Diaspora. While the categorizations overlap, they are distinct from one another. In 586 BC, the Israelites in Judah were exiled to Babylon. There, they lived as exiles in a foreign land until approximately forty-five years later, when King Cyrus allowed the Jews to return to Judah.

On the other hand, the Diaspora describes those who chose to (or had to) remain abroad. The word *Diaspora* comes from the Greek word "to scatter."[6] After the exile, the Jews had literally been scattered across the Persian Empire. The term refers to the voluntary scattering or dispersion of the Jewish people throughout the ancient world.

While Mordecai and Esther's ancestors were forced out of their homeland as exiles, those who later remained abroad, even after King Cyrus allowed them to return, were Diaspora. The difference between the two is important because it helps us understand who was temporarily (albeit, some for decades) displaced versus who permanently changed addresses.

When we study Esther, we study the Diaspora— those who permanently stayed in a foreign culture.

When we study books such as Ezra and Nehemiah, we study the exiles who returned to Jerusalem. When we study Esther, we study the Diaspora—those who permanently stayed in a foreign culture. The distinction is important because it shows us both God's activity in the lives of those who lived in the land of promise—rebuilding the temple, restoring God's Word to the city, and rebuilding Jerusalem's walls in their homeland—and His activity in the lives of those living in secular societies. Esther, who married a Gentile king, and Mordecai, who worked in a pagan empire, fit into that latter category. We can learn much about God's activity and faithfulness in our own lives when studying both the exiles and the Diaspora.

Salt *and* Light *or* Assimilation

ESTHER 2:8-11

My sister Katie married an American who is full-blooded Italian. Her husband's paternal grandparents, the Gattos (Italian for cat), immigrated from Sicily to New Jersey. Wanting to fit into their surroundings, they swapped a few letters of their surname and changed it to Gates. (I secretly lament my sister isn't Katie Gatto because not calling her Katie Cat all these years feels like a missed opportunity.) I recently met an elderly woman with the last name Gates and told her the origins of my sister's last name. My new acquaintance told me her parents had immigrated from Germany with the last name Gersch, and they too changed their name to Gates. It is not without irony that, for many foreigners coming to America, adopting the name Gates was a *gate*way to assimilation.

As the Persian empire occupied more and more territories, people like the Jews often left behind their Hebrew names for Persian ones, whether by choice or assignment (Dan. 1:6-7). The name *Mordecai* incorporates the name *Marduk*, which is the state god of Babylon.[7] The name *Esther* comes from the Persian root word *stâra*, meaning "star," and is linked to the name of a Babylonian goddess.[8]

> **FILL IN THE BLANK** from yesterday's reading in verse 7. Esther's Hebrew name is _____ and means "myrtle."

Oftentimes, Israelite women in the Old Testament were given names of plants, so Hadassah is not unusual.[9] **LOOK UP ISAIAH 41:19 AND 55:13.** Where did God promise that the myrtle would grow and what kind of growth would it replace?

The symbolism in these prophecies foreshadows God's forgiveness and acceptance of His people. Jews today still carry the myrtle in processions at the Feast of Tabernacles, signifying peace and thanksgiving.[10] (I suddenly have the urge to find myrtle-print wallpaper for my guest bath. Apparently, I've been in the book of Esther a wee bit long.) Esther's possession of two names, each from different cultures and backgrounds, "implies a person's moving between two worlds."[11] The name *Hadassah* anchored the queen to God's promises to Israel; the name *Esther* allowed her to move inconspicuously about the culture in which she found herself. This tension—feeling as though you embody too much of the culture you were born into for the one you're living in and vice-versa—isn't just the plight of foreigners; it's the status of the believer.

Personal Reflection: Where or how does your faith in Christ cause you to feel "between two worlds"?

READ ESTHER 2:1-4,8-11.

After Esther was gathered with the other women at the fortress of Susa, where was she taken (v. 8)?

Detail everything we're told about Esther's environment, the people around her, and her daily life (v. 9).

What does verse 11 imply about Mordecai's concern for Esther?

According to verse 9, from what two people did Esther gain favor?

The word *favor* or *kindness* in verse 9 is translated from the Hebrew word *hesed*.[12] It's an important biblical word that often expresses God's covenant love for His people. This same word is used throughout the Old Testament, notably in two other similar and significant stories where God's people find themselves as foreigners in faraway lands.

COMPARE GENESIS 39:20-23 AND DANIEL 1:1-16. Read these passages, then fill in the chart below.

	MAIN CHARACTER	WHO SHOWED HIM FAVOR?	WHAT DID FAVOR LOOK LIKE?
GENESIS 39:20-23			
DANIEL 1:1-16			

Personal Take: What do the passages in Genesis and Daniel reveal about how, and through whom, God can show His children favor?

Turn back to Esther. What does the author tell us about why Esther gained Hegai's favor (circle below)?

| She revealed her Jewishness | She was dutiful | He doesn't give a reason | God intervened |

Personal Reflection: Describe a time when you sensed God's distinct favor in a specific situation. How did you know it was Him and not just a random happening?

LOOK BACK AT ESTHER 2:10. TRUE OR FALSE? Mordecai encouraged Esther to boldly proclaim her Jewish heritage to Hegai no matter the cost.

In Joseph's and Daniel's stories we can readily see both their courageous obedience and God's unmistakable hand of *hesed* or *favor* on their lives. However, in Esther's story, the favor she receives can't be directly connected to any faith-act on her part, nor is God explicitly mentioned.

Personal Take: Why do you think Esther was shown favor despite no mention of God, and no mention of her mentioning God (unlike Daniel)?

We'll talk more about God's favor tomorrow, because the word will show up again. What I want you to see today is that both Esther and Mordecai appear to be somewhat assimilated into the Persian culture. Esther was a Persian as far as anyone was concerned. However, the lack of an explicit stand for her faith doesn't mean her heart wasn't there.

At the same time, we can still note the differences between Esther and people like Joseph and Daniel. As Bible students, we easily expect God's *hesed* to show up for the overtly faithful and courageous. We don't as often look for it to be poured out on the vulnerable, the scared, perhaps even the weak in faith. It turns out that complicated isn't too much for God's *hesed*.

Let's fast-forward about five hundred years to a message Jesus gave His disciples early in His ministry.

READ MATTHEW 5:13-16 BELOW, and underline what Jesus called His followers to be.

You are the salt of the earth. But if the salt should lose its taste, how can it be made salty? It's no longer good for anything but to be thrown out and trampled under people's feet. You are the light of the world. A city situated on a hill cannot be hidden.

No one lights a lamp and puts it under a basket, but rather on a lampstand, and it gives light for all who are in the house. In the same way, let your light shine before others, so that they may see your good works and give glory to your Father in heaven.

When we actively do good out of love for others, who is to receive the glory (v. 16)?

Personal Take: What is it about salt and light that makes it impossible for them to blend in?

SALT	LIGHT

In antiquity, salt was used to heal and cleanse, but one of its main purposes was to preserve meat by slowing down decay. Followers of Christ are to be people who push back the decay in our world. At the same time, we are to dispel the darkness with the light of the gospel. Salt is defensive, and light is offensive, but both are distinct from their surroundings!

Mordecai and Esther's decision for her to blend into the Persian culture and to conceal her Jewish identity in the harem was complicated at the very least. It's unlikely any of us will ever face anything close. Today, our call is much clearer. We are to openly bear witness to Christ, to spread the good news of His gospel even when it costs us.

GOSPEL MOMENT

As salt and light, how are we to be distinct from, but engaged with, our world?

Personal Response:

What makes your life distinct from those around you who don't have the hope of Christ? Or, does your life look the same as everyone else's? A little different? A lot different?

What is one action step you can take to be more salt and light?

Much like Christ followers today, Israel was to be set apart from the world. They were to be a distinct people for God's renown. No matter where they found themselves living, God's people were to infiltrate and impact their surrounding culture, not in spite of their different way of life but because of it. Neither biblical accounts nor history tell us much about what religious life looked like for the Jewish population in Susa. Yet, Esther's account tells us that God had not forgotten His people. Today we can bear witness to a Jewish woman named Esther, in a faraway fortress, whom God is about to call out from among her peers in unmistakable fashion. May He do the same for us.

God's Favor *in* Complexity

ESTHER 2:12-18

I hosted my niece Harper's birthday celebration at my house with several of her fifth-grade girlfriends. As an aunt without children of my own, I welcome a Friday night where my back porch is crawling with soon-to-be sixth-graders. One of my duties was recording what child gave Harper what gift because my sister-in-law Megen will not forget a thank-you note. Three presents in, I had lost all track. I was in a sea of cosmetics, scrambling for who gave the lip gloss and blush, who wrapped the cuticle lotion, and who brought the makeup blender sponge set, which, incidentally, I had never heard of before. This was the night when I came to understand that eleven is the new fourteen. It was also a reminder that beauty will forever be big business because it's one of our deepest cravings.

Earlier, I pointed out that, when studying the Bible, it's important to understand how ancient cultural customs differ from our own. It's equally important to notice where things have stayed remarkably the same. The Persian empire might not have had department stores lined with cosmetic counters, but its inhabitants were trailblazers of the spa, essential oils, and facials. A woman's beauty was prized in Persia as much as it is in Hollywood—and apparently in the fifth grade.

READ ESTHER 2:12-14.

How long did the beauty treatment last before a concubine would be taken to the king?

What specific beauty elements and processes are mentioned?

When a woman from the harem was summoned, what was she allowed to bring with her?

Persia was known for its aromatic perfumes and was a large exporter of them. Archaeologists have unearthed beautifying treatments that prepared a bride for her wedding.[13] They've uncovered cosmetic burners that fumigate myrrh for both hygienic and therapeutic purposes.[14] At face value, twelve months spent in a luxurious palace, breathing and soaking in every imaginable essential oil, while beauticians plump lips and lift eyelids, massage your feet and steep your afternoon tea, sounds lovely. (Don't mind me bringing my own needs and imagination to the scene.)

The problem with this elaborate year-long treatment (among many) is that, though it was done *to* the women, it wasn't done *for* them. The chief end of their beautifying process was meeting the insatiable sexual desires of the king. And, for many of them, for one night only (Esth. 2:14).

> **LOOK BACK AT THE END OF VERSE 14.** What was the plight of the majority of women who spent the night with the king?

Perhaps being selected into the harem was at first alluring—a thrilling chance to be queen. The desperate reality, however, is that all but one were looking at a life-sentence of isolation and loneliness. For most, the hope of being queen ended in something more akin to widowhood than marriage.[15]

> Personal Reflection: What other examples in our world hold out the promise of fulfillment but end in crushing disappointment or loneliness? Put another way, what experiences, possessions, or achievements do we often scramble and fight for that eventually leave us empty or dissatisfied?

> **LOOK UP PROVERBS 31:30.** How is this verse an encouragement or a challenge to you as we, too, live in a beauty-obsessed culture?

When I was growing up, one prominent speaker at the time said we should never compliment children on their outward appearance—only on their character. This didn't sit right with me then, and if you knew how many times I call each of my nieces *my little princess,* or each of my nephews *the handsomest boy ever,* you would know my thinking hasn't changed. While character and heart are, of course, superior to one's physical appearance, this doesn't mean beauty is insignificant. God created us as physical beings with innate beauty. One of the defining features of our faith is that God made every human being in His very image (Gen. 1:26-27). Our physical bodies and appearances are His creation. Yes, we can make too much of beauty, but we can also make too little of it. As we study a kingdom unhealthily obsessed with a woman's physical splendor, we need not throw the baby out with the bathwater.

Personal Reflection: What does a healthy, God-honoring understanding of beauty entail? How can you take care of yourself, without it consuming you?

READ ESTHER 2:15-18.

What did Esther request to take to the king when she was summoned?

What did Esther gain from the king more than anyone else? (Hint: The same word is used in verse nine from yesterday).

Personal Take: What is your reaction to Esther being made queen? Do you have hopeful expectations, deep reservations, or both? Explain your thoughts.

The king summoned Esther in the month of Tebeth, a cold and wet month in Persia (in Nashville, we know this as February). He crowned her queen during the seventh year of his reign, approximately four years after he deposed Vashti. In between Vashti's and Esther's queenship, history tells us that Ahasuerus suffered mortifying defeats against

Greece that depleted his wealth and pride. It seems his advisors were looking to cheer him up when they suggested he search for a new queen from an assembly of young and beautiful women.[16]

Passages of Scripture like this one can be hard for us to wrap our minds around. I've spent the better part of the day attempting to pull together some semblance of a theological offering from today's verses. I keep finding my face in my palms. I've stepped away from writing more times than a child comes down the stairs for a glass of water after being put to bed. I even rinsed off the bottoms of my feet because they'd gotten a little dirty from walking barefoot to my garden beds to pull weeds, because I've gotten up to do that too.

Esther's path to the crown is complicated and littered with injustices. Women aren't supposed to live in harems. Kings aren't supposed to abusively impose their will on innocent young virgins. And Jewish girls weren't supposed to sleep with men who weren't their husbands, much less Gentile ones![17] Yet, here in the middle of all that is religiously convoluted, that biblical word *favor*, freighted with hope and promise, is showing up where it doesn't belong. Or does it? Perhaps this is exactly the place we should expect to find God's *hesed* for His people.

> **Personal Reflection:** Is there a situation in your life that is messy and complicated? How does today's passage encourage you that God is still able to intervene and redeem?

Now that Esther has been crowned queen, some of you may be wondering about Vashti. Sadly, we don't hear of Vashti again, and we don't know what happened to her. But as a friend insightfully shared, if Vashti hadn't resisted the king's summons, Esther wouldn't have ascended to the place she is at now, and an entire people group would have suffered.

Compare and contrast Vashti and Esther below (Vashti is mentioned in 1:9-12, if you need to look back). There may not be a lot of information to go on, but note every similarity and difference you find.

SIMILARITIES	DIFFERENCES

We are not told Vashti's motives for refusing the king's wicked demands, nor are we told Esther's for going along with them. But most importantly, we must see Esther and Vashti as Jew and Gentile. We must keep in the forefront of our minds God's covenant with His people, the Jews. Esther's rising in the ranks of the Persian empire is not a result of her choices; rather, it's about God's faithfulness. Yes, even to those scattered across the Persian empire, who most certainly were wondering if they were still the people of God.

READ ISAIAH 41:8-14. Here, the prophet Isaiah encourages the exiles.

What had God not done to His scattered people (v. 9)?

List all of God's promises in verses 9-10.

What name is God called in addition to "Lord" and "Holy One" in verse 14?

Messiah   King   Ruler   Redeemer

It would be nice to think that lustful men in power, harems, and beauty-obsessed cultures have been lost to the days of antiquity, but we're not that naïve. Still, God is our Redeemer in the middle of it all. The word *redeem* means to buy back from bondage or avenge someone from wrongdoing.[18] All the way in Persia, in the middle of abuse and oppression, God would put His hand on a young woman, an orphan and an exile, and give her favor.

I pray that no matter where you find yourself today, you will know that the favor of the Lord is upon you (Ps. 84:11).

An Age-Old Rivalry

ESTHER 2:19-23; 3:1-6

Do you ever wonder what would have happened if you'd been born into a different family? Or where you would have ended up if you went to a different college, or took a different job out of high school, or were late to the barbecue where you met your best friend or your future husband? One evening, I parked my car in the street instead of in my friend's driveway where I normally park. Later that night, a woman on her way home accidentally swiped the side of my car, resulting in a minor fender-bender. She was distressed, as anyone would be. My friends and I helped her get home, we've stayed in touch, and several months later she has become a friend. What if I had parked where I normally do instead of on the street? She never would have hit my car—typically the outcome I'm shooting for—but I would also be short a new friend.

I can't begin to unravel the mysteries of God's providence, why His hand is hidden in one instance and as obvious as if He had reached it right out of the sky in others. If the book of Esther is known for anything, it is for revealing God's actions without mentioning Him. Irony is its hallmark. Nearly every happening in this short book, no matter how normal, eventually turns out to be extremely not normal. But I'm saying too much. Let's start reading.

READ ESTHER 2:19-22.

Where was Mordecai when Esther and the rest of the concubines were gathered (circle below)?

In the city   At the King's Gate   In the temple   Back in Jerusalem

What is at least one reason why Esther kept her Jewish identity concealed (v. 20)?

Who were Bigthan and Teresh, and what were they conspiring to do?

When Mordecai heard of the eunuchs' plot, who did he report it to?

Personal Take: Mordecai and Esther were working together in matters of life and death. In our modern world, where both male dominance and radical feminism coexist, how do you already see Mordecai and Esther's relationship as different from either one of these positions?

If Mordecai was in the right *place* at the right time, Esther was in the right *position* at the right time. Both needed to be exactly where they were to spare the king. Yet, neither seems to have any idea of how God is using their positions or partnership. They are seemingly unaware of God's providence in their lives, as we so often are.

The term *providence* is a central theme of the book of Esther and an important doctrine of our Christian faith (see p. 62). It's the reality that God is in control of all things and active in our everyday lives. Consider the following definitions from various Bible dictionaries.

PROVIDENCE IS:

"God's care over creation and his control of history."[19]

"God's faithful and effective care and guidance of everything which He has made toward the end which He has chosen."[20]

"The sovereign, divine superintendence of all things, guiding them toward their divinely predetermined end in a way that is consistent with their created nature, all to the glory and praise of God."[21]

Personal Take: Based on these definitions, and your knowledge of Scripture, craft your own definition of God's providence.

Personal Reflection: How does the concept of providence bring comfort and peace to your life? Think specifically about God's providence in challenging or distressing seasons where you can't understand what's going on or what He's doing.

READ ESTHER 3:1-6.

Today, a new, and very bad, no-good character is introduced. His name is Haman, son of Hammedatha the _____.

The king promoted Haman, even though it was Mordecai who foiled the plot to kill the king. We are not told why Haman was promoted, but the detail is meant to surprise us since learning of Mordecai's promotion-worthy deed. Regardless of whether Mordecai was overlooked or forgotten about, we will soon see that God's providence was at work.

Ahasuerus commanded the royal staff who served at the King's Gate to bow down to Haman. Why did Mordecai refuse (circle below)?

| He was mad about not getting Haman's position | He had religious reasons | We're not told | He wanted to be like Daniel |

To best understand the book of Esther we must allow the rest of the Old Testament to be its chief commentary. Haman was an Agagite. The Agagites were descendants of King Agag, who ruled the Amalekites. You will remember from Day 1 of this week that Mordecai was a Benjamite, the son of Kish. This linked Mordecai to Israel's first king, King Saul. King Agag ruled during King Saul's reign over Israel. Early in Saul's reign the Lord told him to attack the Amalekites and wipe them out completely. Saul disobeyed the Lord and destroyed only what he deemed invaluable, keeping back the best of the plunder, including King Agag (1 Sam. 15).

READ DEUTERONOMY 25:17-19. What do we learn about the Amalekites and their destiny?

READ EXODUS 17:8-16. According to verse 16, who did the Amalekites ultimately oppose?

That Haman is an Agagite makes him an unmistakable enemy of the Jews. In modern-day terms the characterization is akin to being a Nazi. Mordecai and Haman aren't merely Jew and Gentile, they represent a long-standing rivalry between Israel and her worst enemies. This is why many scholars see Mordecai's refusal to bow before Haman as springing from "tribal enmity" more than religious conviction.[22] Furthermore, this type of bowing had to do with respect, not worship.[23] The members of the royal staff eventually outed Mordecai for not bowing down, as well as for being a Jew. Although Persia as a whole was known for its tolerance of diverse people groups and their beliefs, antisemitism still resided in the hearts of certain individuals, Haman being chief among them.

Compare Haman's reaction to Mordecai with Ahasuerus's reaction to Vashti when she refused to show off her beauty (1:13-22). What similarities do you see?

Not only were Haman and Ahasuerus both filled with rage, both extended the wrath of their anger beyond the person who refused them. Vashti *and* all the women of Persia suffered as a result of Ahasuerus's anger. Mordecai *and* all the Jews were threatened with genocide as a result of Haman's rage.

Personal Reflection: Has a long-standing prejudice or rivalry taken root in your heart? Are you allowing past wounds or offenses to keep you bitter, angry, or unforgiving? Journal below and confess these to the Lord.

The bitterness between the Israelites and Amalekites was as old as time. Enduring rivalries like these don't die easily. Racism and prejudice are prime examples of how animosity can travel through generations. Sometimes, though, our conflicts begin by simply allowing untended hurt to pile on top of untended hurt. We let disagreements turn to full-blown fights, which can then turn into silence and eventual estrangement. Because of Christ, we are offered a better way.

GOSPEL MOMENT

READ COLOSSIANS 3:1-17. Here, Paul wrote about taking off the old, putting on the new, and what reconciled relationships look like in Him.

Personal Response: What is one piece of "old clothing" you can take off today? What new piece can you put on?

Ahasuerus and Haman may be extreme examples of the damaging effects of pride, jealousy, and anger, but we can't underestimate the damage these sins do to others and our own hearts. As we watch the folly and danger of the Persian empire play out, we will witness the atrocities the human heart is capable of when unwilling to bow to the Living God. Today is a good day for us to bow our heads before the Lord and confess that He is God and we are not. To confess that we want no part with Haman or Ahasuerus. We want to be clothed in the righteousness of Christ. To be at peace with one another so far as it lies within our power. Anchoring ourselves in this unwavering truth brings peace and comfort, especially when our circumstances are troubling.

I have some friends who have fostered a baby boy for the past year. They brought him home when he was only nine days old. They would love nothing more than to adopt this child as their own. Knowing their love for him and their relentless passion to keep him, I was recently moved by their faith in God's providence over their own understanding. The baby's foster mother said, "We can't claim to know what is best for our child. Only God knows, and we want His will." This is what it means to rest in the providence of God. May His powerful provision and loving preservation minister to your heart today.

God's PROVIDENCE

The idea of God's providence is synonymous with His provision for us. Notice *providence* includes the word *provide*. The word also includes ideas of foresight and forethought. In our limited capacity, we make provision for our lives based on what we are able to see coming. We may set aside money for a child's college tuition, prepare for an upcoming work presentation, or put ourselves in the best position to succeed physically and spiritually. We are wise to look ahead and provide for ourselves and for others accordingly. But our foresight and resources are limited. Not only are we unable to see the future perfectly, we don't always know what God's perfect will is for our lives or for others. This is where God's providence comes in.

No matter what we face in our lives, God is lovingly in control.

God knows what we need, can see the future perfectly, and knows where all of life is headed; He is the One who guides and guards our lives. Isn't it a comforting thought that no matter what we face in our lives, God is lovingly in control? Not only does He hold us fast, but He also guides our steps in keeping with His loving will. He is both directing our individual lives and the world at large. He is moving all things toward the full accomplishment of His purposes. We can rest in His bountiful providence.

One of the hallmarks of the book of Esther is this theme of God's providence. While God's name is never mentioned, the work of His hand is visible at every turn. Mordecai's position in the royal court and Esther's place in the royal palace are evidence of God's divine placement and appointment. Mordecai overhearing the plot to assassinate the king and working with Esther to foil it were providential circumstances that played a role in the future deliverance of the Jews. God also fashioned seemingly mundane details such as Haman's gallows and the king's sleepless night to accomplish His purpose—the saving of the Jews.

Ultimately, God's providence throughout the Old Testament moves toward the coming Messiah, Jesus Christ. For us today, God's providence is moving us toward holy living, love for one another, fruitfulness in Christ, and our eternal home in heaven. We can rest in the truth that God is not only the Creator of the universe but the Preserver of it as well.

The Apple of God's Eye

ESTHER 3:7-15

Yesterday we left off with Haman's plan to annihilate the Jews in the Persian Empire, which would have accounted for every living Jew at the time. While we might expect Haman's gross overreaction to dissipate with a good night's sleep, this is far too reasonable of an assumption—Haman's pride knows no bounds. His plans of genocide begin to take serious and seemingly irreversible shape in today's passage.

READ ESTHER 3:7-9.

Casting lots was a common practice in the ancient world. The lot, or *pûr*, was a small clay cube, and it was thrown the way we roll dice. The lot was cast to determine fate and destiny. This was a custom particularly associated with the New Year period in Persia.[24] We'll understand more about why the lot was cast before Haman later in today's study.

What complaints did Haman bring to the king about the Jews (v. 8)? List everything he mentions.

TRUE OR FALSE? Haman does not mention the Jews by name when addressing the king.

Personal Take: We've already learned that Esther assimilated into the harem and kept her Jewish identity a secret. We also know that both Mordecai and Esther helped save the king's life. How do these details contradict some of what Haman accused the Jewish people of?

One of my seminary professors, Dr. Craig Blomberg, notes Haman's deceptive progression in verse 8. Haman begins with truth about the Jewish people (they were dispersed throughout the kingdom), to half-truth (they separate themselves; don't follow customs), to full lie (they don't obey the king's laws).[25] We have no reason to believe that the dispersed Jews didn't obey the laws of the land—for one thing, Mordecai foiled a plot to assassinate the king! For the Jewish people, one of the attractive aspects of the Persian Empire was its tolerance of ethnic minorities and their customs. It's one of the reasons why so many Jews stayed where they were instead of returning to Jerusalem.[26] Haman was propagating lies and stirring up prejudice.

> What was Haman willing to deposit into the royal treasury for Ahasuerus's stamp of approval to carry out his plan against the Jews?

The 375 tons of silver was an absurd amount of money, approximately two-thirds of a year's revenue from the whole empire.[27] No matter the exact amount of silver, the message is clear: money talks. Given the king's recent setback of losing big to Greece, it seems that money might have been talking even louder than normal.

> **READ ESTHER 3:10-15.**
>
> Describe the orders sent to the officials of every people group in the empire and translated into each language, according to verse 13.

> Let's get our bearings on the timeline of Haman's decree. On the calendar months below, circle the days of the following two events: 1. The day the decree was written (v. 12). 2. The day of the attack on the Jews (v. 13).

NISAN, THE 1ST MONTH

ADAR, THE 12TH MONTH

The *pûr* was thrown in the first month of Nisan, and the decree to destroy the Jews was written on the thirteenth of that month. But the date to which the lot fell was the thirteenth day of the last month of the year. In other words, Haman threw the *pûr* for a "lucky result," but what he got was a date eleven months later, leaving plenty of time for the Jews to prepare.

Proverbs 16:33 says, "The lot is cast into the lap, but its every decision is from the Lord." The New Living Translation of the Bible puts it like this, "We may throw the dice, but the Lord determines how they fall."

Personal Reflection: Early on in Esther's story, we see God's sovereignty at work. How does this encourage you in a world where so much can seem left to chance?

Since we will be seeing these months again, it's helpful to know that on the Hebrew calendar, Adar corresponds with February–March and Nisan with March–April. For the Jewish reader of the time, the thirteenth day of the first month, Nisan, was immediately recognizable as the day before Passover (Lev. 23:5)!

READ EXODUS 23:15 AND DEUTERONOMY 16:1-8. Why did the Jews celebrate Passover? (Note: Aviv or Abib became Nisan in the post-exilic age.)

Put yourself in the shoes of the Diaspora (Jewish people living in Persia). You receive the news that Ahasuerus is decreeing the annihilation of your family, friends, and entire people group on the very day you are to begin a week of celebrating God's deliverance of your ancestors from Egypt. In other words, the day that marks your people becoming a nation under God's covenant is the day that will mark the total extinction of your people (an event to happen in eleven months).

Personal Reflection: What are you thinking if you're a Jew in Persia? Are you trusting God's promises to your people will prevail in seemingly irreversible circumstances? Do you assume God has given up on you because, after all, you are living so far from the land He promised you and your ancestors? Share your thoughts.

Personal Take: What does the second half of verse 15 tell you about the king and Haman, and their relationship to the people they were supposed to be looking out for?

How is Haman son of Hammedatha the Agagite described in verse 10?

Power hungry   Racist   Prideful   Enemy of the Jews

The Hiding Place, the masterful story of Corrie ten Boom, a Dutch Christian who helped her family hide Jews during World War II, recounts a moment Corrie had with her father before both of their looming imprisonments.

> *One day as Father and I were returning from our walk we found the Grote Markt cordoned off by a double ring of police and soldiers. A truck was parked in front of the fish mart; into the back were climbing men, women, and children, all wearing the yellow star. . . .*
>
> *"Father! Those poor people!" I cried . . .*
>
> *"Those poor people," Father echoed. But to my surprise I saw that he was looking at the soldiers now forming into ranks to march away. "I pity the poor Germans, Corrie. They have touched the apple of God's eye."[28]*

Corrie's father understood the terrible fate of the Nazis, those who dared torture God's very own. A millennium before this unfathomable scene in Haarlem, Holland, Haman and Ahasuerus clinked glasses together, drunk on wine and absolute power, while the city of Susa and the Jewish people were thrown into chaos and horror. Who is to be pitied?

I can't help but close our week by looking at another event that took place on the eve of Passover.

READ JOHN 13:1.

GOSPEL MOMENT

As Christ followers, we must view the chaos in Persia on the eve of Passover in light of the once-and-for-all sacrifice of the Lamb of God. We will explore this further in the days to come. But for now, remember that, much like the Diaspora, we can't always understand what God is doing, how He will do what He has promised, or when He will do it.

Personal Reflection: What difficult or perplexing situation do you find yourself in? What questions do you have about God's faithfulness to you? Take some time to pray over these questions and offer them to Him. You are the apple of His eye.

So many in our world still abuse power and toast themselves while the poor and powerless suffer. But unlike the Diaspora, we live in the reality of God's kingdom having come to earth in Jesus. God now passes over our sin because of Christ's once-and-for-all sacrifice on our behalf. And as a result, we have the Holy Spirit who has given us the power to be salt and light in our dark world.

We can also take heart that God's providence is active in our lives. Though not one miracle is mentioned in the book of Esther, by the time you add up all the moments of "happenstance" that result in divine rescue, you can't help but throw your hands up in the air and exclaim, *Only God!* A series of ordinary events under God's hand become extraordinary to say the least—some might even say miraculous. Take courage that His Spirit is with you now. He loves you, is for you, and His favor rests upon you.

Spring Asparagus Fettuccine

I love to cook seasonally whenever I can. Springtime kicks off the fresh produce season, and nothing says spring like asparagus. My dear friend Regina Pinto, who I wrote my cookbook A Place at the Table *with, shared this recipe. I made it and instantly knew it had to go in this study. It's fresh. It's light. It's delicious. And you get your vegetable servings.*

INGREDIENTS

- 15 oz. package fettuccine pasta
- 15 medium-thick asparagus, blanched
- 2 Tbs butter
- 2 Tbs olive oil
- 3 garlic cloves, finely chopped or crushed
- 1 Tbs lemon zest
- ½ cup pine nuts toasted (broil in oven on pan but be careful to watch they don't burn)
- 1 ½ cups parmesan cheese, grated (½ cup set aside for topping)
- ½ cup finely chopped fresh basil
- Salt and pepper to taste

DIRECTIONS

1. Boil pasta al dente according to directions and drain. Blanch asparagus (after water is boiling add asparagus for 2-3 minutes until cooked, then remove). After asparagus have cooled, cut them lengthwise into thin strips like the pasta noodles.

2. In a large pan, melt butter until almost brown. Add pasta, asparagus, garlic, lemon zest, toasted pine nuts, 1 cup parmesan, and basil. Toss in pan with olive oil (add more oil if needed).

3. Serve with grilled chicken or salmon and sprinkle with additional parmesan cheese.

Watch the Session Three Video

Use the space below to follow along with the outline points from Kelly's teaching. A leader guide is available for free download at **lifeway.com/estherstudy.**

1. Even in the _____ and _____ corners of the world, God is _____.

2. _____ thrives on the work of a billion-dollar industry. _____ is the work of the Spirit.

3. Esther's *outward* beauty may have been her _____ _____, but it was her *inward* beauty that God would use _____.

4. If God can show up in the middle of a harem, _____ _____?

5. King Jesus _____ you and He _____ you by name.

To access the video sessions, use the instructions in the back of your Bible study book.

For

Such a Time as This

SESSION FOUR

$\mathcal{A}$ Day of Lament

ESTHER 4:1-3

Today is a day of lament in our story of Esther. *Lament* is an important concept throughout the Bible, but it's an idea we don't often think about in day-to-day life. A lament is in an expression, usually verbal (like weeping or expressing grief) or physical (like the tearing of clothes), that is done "to express profound sorrow" or "to mourn passionately."[1] It's an invitation to share with God and others our feelings of deep pain and the emotional rawness brought about by life's trials.

I realize this is not the "funnest" way to begin a week of Bible study. Lament is not a concept we give much time or thought to these days, even in many of our churches. I can see why it's not optimal to kick off a Sunday morning worship set with songs about how painful life can be and how hard it is to trust the Lord. But the truth is, we feel like this sometimes. And it's important to know that, throughout Scripture, God invites our questions, doubts, tears, and mourning. He never asks us to ignore our pain. In fact, Scripture talks about the benefits of lamenting in God's presence.

The author of Ecclesiastes put it this way,

> *It is better to go to a house of mourning than to go to a house of feasting, since that is the end of all mankind, and the living should take it to heart. Grief is better than laughter, for when a face is sad, a heart may be glad. The heart of the wise is in a house of mourning, but the heart of fools is in a house of pleasure.*
>
> *ECCLESIASTES 7:2-4*

While we don't want to make the house of mourning our permanent dwelling, we do need to visit there when it's appropriate. When we minimize the pain and tragedies of life, we miss the treasures of what it means to love and follow Christ in a broken world. Perhaps today is a day of bringing your grief to the Lord as an act of worship. Sometimes, lamenting in God's presence is the most fitting worship we can bring Him because it's the most authentic worship we have.

READ ESTHER 4:1-3.

Verse 1 is filled with descriptions about Mordecai's reaction to the king's edict. Write down the following observations:

What did Mordecai do to his clothes?

What did he put on?

Where did he go?

What did he do when he got there?

According to verse 3, where was there mourning among the Jews?

REFER BACK TO MAP OF PERSIA ON PAGE 23

Did you notice the Jews mourned in *every province*? This even includes the exiles who had returned to Jerusalem to be part of its rebuilding. Remember, the edict didn't only apply to the Jews in the capital of Susa, but to the entire Persian empire, which included Jerusalem! The edict applied to every Jew alive at the time. Their intense display of mourning makes sense. Tearing one's clothes, putting on sackcloth, and sprinkling oneself with ashes was a way of showing extreme grief.[2] It was often accompanied by other dramatic expressions, as mentioned in verse 3.

Verse 3 says the people _____, _____, and _____.

When considering this idea of lament, my friend Haley said, "We talk to our friends when we're in pain, why would we not talk to God?" What we see in verse 3 is a group of people going to God in their devastation.

Personal Reflection: Are you more likely to: A) weep in the Lord's presence over a loss, a disappointment, or something that's grieved you; or, B) deal with it yourself, push it down, or keep it separate from your relationship with God? Explain.

Sometimes, we get the impression that "good" Christians should always be happy no matter what and that mourning and bewilderment don't belong in the lives of those who have victory in Jesus. But this isn't so. Even Jesus Himself cried out on the cross, "My God, My God, why have you forsaken me?" (Matt. 27:46, NIV). The psalmists and prophets despaired before the Lord, and Paul wrote that while we don't mourn without hope, we do still mourn (1 Thess. 4:13). The Jews in Esther's day were right to be overwrought with despair. They were right to do what the people of God have done for generations: fast, weep, and mourn.

As we consider biblical lament, it's helpful to know that it can be practiced both personally and corporately. Also, we can lament for various reasons—the loss of a loved one, injustice, physical suffering, and sin, to name a few. But lament is not simply complaining or despairing. As one author puts it, lament is "a prayer of pain that leads to trust."[3] It is bringing our sorrow and anguish before God because we believe He is powerful, merciful, and good, even when we can't make sense of our circumstances. Even when trusting Him seems counterintuitive.

One of the best places to see a variety of lamentation in the Bible is in the book of Psalms. In fact, lament makes up the biggest category of psalms! Let's look at three specific psalms of lament before returning to Esther.

READ PSALM 10:1-2,12-18; PSALM 13:1-6; AND PSALM 51:1-12 and fill in the chart on the following page.

	PSALM 10:1-2, 12-18	PSALM 13:1-6	PSALM 51:1-12
WHAT IS TROUBLING THE PSALMIST?			
IS HE TROUBLED PRIMARILY FOR HIMSELF OR OTHERS?			
WHAT ATTRIBUTES AND ACTIONS OF GOD COMFORT HIM?			

In each of these psalms, we see the intimacy that happens when we pour out our longings, questions, and fears to the Lord. I believe this is why Paul wrote that he longed to know the power of Christ's resurrection and the fellowship of His sufferings (Phil. 3:10). There's a unique fellowship that comes when we walk with Jesus in times of trial. Lament is its own special form of worship.

READ THE FOLLOWING OLD TESTAMENT VERSES.

When I heard these words, I sat down and wept. I mourned for a number of days, fasting and praying before the God of the heavens.

NEHEMIAH 1:4

Yet when they were sick, my clothing was sackcloth; I humbled myself with fasting, and my prayer was genuine.

PSALM 35:13

So I turned my attention to the Lord God to seek him by prayer and petitions, with fasting, sackcloth, and ashes.

DANIEL 9:3

Now look back at the blanks you filled in from Esther 4:3 near the top of today's study. What is noticeably missing from the list of activities coupled with fasting?

While prayer is not mentioned in the book of Esther, there is good reason to assume that prayer also accompanied the Jews' fasting, weeping, and mourning. Turn forward in your Bible to the prophetic book of Joel. In chapter 2, the prophet calls God's people to repentance. Though not all lament has to do with sin, in this case the people were mourning over having turned their backs on God.

READ JOEL 2:12-13.

What three words do you see in verse 12 that mirror Esther 4:3?
_____, _____, and _____.

What attributes does Joel ascribe to God?

Personal Take: God is more interested in His people tearing their hearts than He is with them tearing their clothes. In your own words, what does "tear your hearts" mean? Why do you think that matters more to God?

I love that our God is personal! I love that He is intimate with us. I love that He is abounding in love. The problem is, we don't often lament long enough to experience the Lord's healing touch. If you're disappointed, let Him know. If you're worried, bring your anxiety to Him. If you have questions, lay them at His feet. If you're in sin, turn to Him and repent. If injustice is plaguing you or your loved-ones, petition our great God.

The people in Esther's day knew who to turn to in times of crisis. While the palace feasted, God's people fasted. While the nobles drank wine to the dregs, the Jews drank from the cup of sorrow. In the end, God's covenant people would have a story to tell of God's faithfulness, while the Persian oppressors would be left with hollow memories of power and pleasure. My friend, if you are in the house of mourning, you have chosen a hard but good place because God is there. He is near to the broken hearted and saves those who are crushed in spirit (Ps. 34:18).

Personal Prayer: Write a prayer of lament below, either for yourself, someone else, or a group of people. Be sure to include attributes of God and a commitment to trust in Him. On the next page, you'll find a hymn of lament to reflect on as you pray.

A pastor in my community recently endured the tragic loss of his only daughter. In the aftermath, he said, "A strong confidence in the end of the story does not undo or justify the absence of grief in the middle. A mature faith adds its tears to the sadness in our world. Jesus said, 'Blessed are those who mourn' all the while not losing confidence in how that sadness will eventually be overcome in Him."[4]

Though we have confidence in how the story will end, the Lord invites us to lament in His presence as trial and hardships come—until His return, when every tear will be wiped away and death will be no more.

OUT OF *the* DEPTHS
I CRY

Out of the depths I cry to you on high;
Lord, hear my call.
Bend down your ear and listen to my sigh,
forgiving all.
If you should mark our sins, who then could stand?
But grace and mercy dwell at your right hand.

I wait for God, I trust his holy word;
he hears my sighs.
My soul still waits and looks unto the Lord;
my prayers arise.
I look for him to drive away my night–
yes, more than those who watch for morning light.

Hope in the Lord: unfailing is his love;
in him confide.
Mercy and full redemption from above
he does provide.
From sin and evil, mighty though they seem,
his arm almighty will his saints redeem.

Source: Psalter, 1912, alt. Public Domain.

An Impossible Situation

ESTHER 4:4-12

The view from my back porch used to include three giant Leyland Cypresses, a towering Oak, and half a Hackberry Tree. The scenery was lush. That is, until one December evening when a hard freeze killed everything. The one pleasant surprise, however, is that I can now see a grand and gorgeously coiffed tree, one with multiple branches fanning outward in near perfect symmetry and crowned with a healthy head of thick, summer-green hair. The pre-existing foliage had obscured my view of this near perfect Maple. In this case, I hadn't been able to see the tree for the forest.

Sometimes, the removal of certain obstacles or distractions, even healthy activities, can sharpen our perspective. Suddenly, what we couldn't see before now towers in front of us with unmistakable clarity. If Esther had, at any time, thought her ascension to the queen's throne was for her own personal glory or pleasure, those branches were about to be lopped off. And if Mordecai's purpose was obstructed by the overgrowth of years of daily life in pagan Persia, all that was about to be pruned back. Soon, God and His purposes would be in clear view for both of them.

READ ESTHER 4:4-12.

What was Esther's emotional response when she heard that Mordecai was wailing in the city while wearing sackcloth and ashes (v. 4)?

What did Esther send Mordecai via Hathach, the king's eunuch?

Money   A letter   A fresh set of clothing   A sword

Esther was overwrought with fear (some versions say "distress"), and I appreciate this detail because it reminds us that she is human. Even queens get scared. It appears she was unaware of the king's edict. She only knew that something truly devastating must have happened for Mordecai to publicly expose his turmoil. We can't know for certain what this exchange entailed, but I can't help but wonder if she sent him clothing so he could enter the King's Gate (4:2). Or, if she was concerned that his sackcloth would tip the Persian court off to his Jewishness—for those who didn't yet know—or worse yet, tip people off to her own.

Back and forth, from palace to court, short messages flew between Esther and Mordecai, like modern text messages. (I'd like to think that if the name *Hathach* had more of a ring to it we'd have a texting app named after him.)

Using your own words, fill in each message below. This exercise will help you feel the magnitude of what was at stake.

(v. 5) Esther sends Hathach to Mordecai to ask . . .

(vv. 7-8) Mordecai sends Hathach to Esther to tell her . . .

(v. 11) Esther sends Hathach back to Modercai to explain . . .

COMPLETE THE FOLLOWING SECTION TOMORROW

(vv. 13-14) Mordecai responds to Esther that . . .

(vv. 15-16) Esther sends a message back to Mordecai commanding him to . . .

Hathach's trustworthy nature plays an important role in the narrative. Without his integrity, the communication between Esther and Mordecai would have been compromised.

> Why was approaching the king uninvited a life-threatening risk for Esther? And when was the last time she was summoned?

Personal Take: Hathach carried out his "behind the scenes" role with excellence. How does his example encourage you in whatever seemingly mundane tasks you're responsible for?

For the first time in the story, we hear directly from Esther (v. 11). She explains that approaching the king means putting her life in jeopardy. The remarks of Jewish scholar Jon Levenson are convicting: Esther is now called upon to risk her life "on behalf of the beleaguered people with whom she has not yet publicly identified." She must go from "a self-styled Persian to a reconnected Jew."5

Personal Reflection: Imagine you're Esther standing at this crossroads. What might have propelled you to stay a "self-styled Persian"? And what would have convicted you to become a "reconnected Jew"?

We don't have to make too big of a leap to see the connection to our own day. How easy it is to keep quiet about our faith in Christ among our colleagues, neighbors, and friends. And yet, will we really serve a Savior with whom we have not yet publicly identified? Will we stand up for our church community when no one knows we're even a part of it?

Certainly, Esther's situation was extreme. It is unlikely that any of us will be forced to put our lives on the line for an entire people group. Yet, how often do we resist speaking up for our faith for fear of our reputations? We're afraid that if we tell our neighbors and coworkers we are followers of Jesus we will be lumped in with religious fanatics or the intellectually weak, thrown into a certain political party, or just labeled a strange ranger. The stakes are higher for some: the loss of a job or professional opportunity, maligned character, or an uncomfortable situation for one's children. The costs are real, and more so by the day.

But sometimes it is these very risks that define the edges of our faith. When compromise is easy to come by, our faith can lose its definition. But when our work, child's school, or social status in the neighborhood comes into direct conflict with being obedient to God's Word, we're suddenly forced to choose. Will we blend in or take a stand? This was the question for Esther, and it's the question for Christ followers today.

READ JOHN 18:12-27.

In verse 17, how did Peter respond to a woman who asked him if he was one of Jesus's disciples?

In verses 25-26, how did Peter respond to the people standing around the fire and one of the high priest's servants?

In between Peter's denials is a short encounter that Jesus had with the high priest Annas. In contrast to Peter, how did Jesus describe the way He had gone about His teaching and ministry?

You and I have the opportunity to talk about the hope we've found in Jesus! Yes, some will dismiss what we have to say, but many are longing for Jesus in their lives. Let's not hold back. We may be afraid, but so was Esther. And as we'll see tomorrow, fear didn't stop her.

LOOK BACK AT ESTHER 2:10 AND 2:20.

Personal Reflection: In light of these verses, why might it be especially difficult for Esther to go to the king for "her people," as Mordecai pleads in Esther 4:8?

Tomorrow we'll study the most well-known verses in the book of Esther. It's everything I can do not to have you jump there now. But I think it's important to sit with Levenson's words while they're still echoing in our souls. Will Esther risk her life for a people she has yet to identify with? And will you and I identify with Christ and His people?

GOSPEL MOMENT

What are some areas of your life where you're hesitant to identify with Christ or His church? (Think about places like your neighborhood or workplace, or around family members you know believe differently.) How can you be more loving and open about your faith in Christ, even when you're afraid to do so?

I've been praying that God would give me natural opportunities to speak about Him without forcing Him into conversations. He has been answering this prayer. Boldness for Christ doesn't *necessarily* mean extremely awkward situations or risk of reputation. It *may* mean those things, but for most of us being a witness for Him is simply a matter of letting our true identity be known—that we love Jesus and follow Him. As we do this, our conversations (as well as the way we walk through life's joys and trials) will naturally testify to His love, authority, and power in our lives.

At the end of this week's study, we'll see Esther determine to stand up for her people. May you and I stand up for Christ and His church with love, truth, and grace.

Who Knows?

ESTHER 4:13-14

Today we're covering the verses which, for centuries, have been the most identifiable from the book of Esther. The phrase, "for such a time as this," is one of Esther's claims to fame. Despite the familiarity, I hope seeing it in context today will help us discover fresh insights into the high-stakes dialogue between Esther and Mordecai. After all, the lives of an entire people group were on the line.

READ ESTHER 4:13-14.

Turn back to page 80 and finish your summarized dialogue between the Queen and Mordecai. Once finished, answer the following questions:

TRUE OR FALSE? Mordecai explained that even though Esther would be spared if she kept silent, it would be the cowardly choice (vv. 13-14).

TRUE OR FALSE? Mordecai was not totally certain that Esther had come to her position "for such a time as this," but he wanted her to consider that this could be the case.

If Esther doesn't step up, deliverance for the Jewish people will:

Never happen	Come from another place	Maybe happen, maybe not	We're not told

Personal Take: Mordecai was clear—Esther would not escape the fate of the Jews just because she was living behind palace walls. Why might Esther have thought she would be exempt from the fate of her people?

In Esther 4:8, Mordecai told Esther to go before the king and beg for mercy on behalf of her people. Obviously, he'd changed his mind about her concealing her Jewish identity. Maybe he thought he'd made a mistake to have asked Esther to cover her identity in the first place, or maybe he recognized that while that was the right choice for a time, it was now time to change course.

> **Personal Reflection:** How has God used a difficult situation in your life to cause you to change your mind about something or simply change course? Explain.

At the end of verse 14, Mordecai said to Esther, "*Who knows, perhaps* you have come to your royal position for such a time as this" (emphasis mine). This statement always feels less than settling to me. If my life and the lives of an entire people group are on the line, I'd be looking for something a little more solid than *who knows?* and *perhaps.* Because we know the end of the story, this statement can feel like a foregone conclusion—surely Esther was the one through whom God would deliver the Jewish people. But in the original language, this sentence is entirely neutral.[6] In other words, Esther's future was anything but certain. We should take Mordecai's words at face value.[7] Maybe Esther was in her position because Almighty God has put her there. One could certainly hope!

> **Personal Reflection:** As believers in Jesus Christ, our calling is certain—we're to love and obey Him. But how the specifics of our calling play out isn't always clear. Is there an area in your life where you're not sure which way to go or which option to choose? Describe it below.

Mordecai and Esther were only a few generations into an unprecedented chapter in Israel's story. What life was supposed to look like for God's covenant people in a place so far away from Jerusalem and how they, as the Diaspora, fit into God's plan, were developing ideas. Would God really use Esther, one whose position came through marriage to a pagan king, whose Jewish identity was unknown? So much about this situation was outside Israel's norm. Mordecai may not have been fully certain about whether God would use Esther, but we can almost see his faith putting the pieces together. If God's covenant was unwavering, why *couldn't* Esther be one of the women God would use to save the Jewish people?

> **Personal Reflection:** Do you ever feel disqualified for God to use you because of parts of your past or how far away from God you've been? How does Esther's unique situation show that God is not only able but willing to step into the hardest, darkest, and farthest places to raise up people for His wonderful purposes?

Mordecai insisted that even if Esther remained silent, deliverance would come to the Jews from another place. This is the closest anyone comes in the book to making a reference to God. The implicit message is that God will deliver His people one way or another. The question is, does Esther want to be part of it? But where did Mordecai get the assurance of this deliverance? Remember, Israel no longer had a king through whom rescue could come. The newly rebuilt temple was small by comparison to Solomon's, and the city of Jerusalem was struggling to get back on its feet. The Jewish people were scattered throughout an empire that had tolerated them up to this point but didn't adhere to their beliefs in God. To answer this question, we have to go back to God's earlier promises to His covenant people.

READ DEUTERONOMY 4:25-31.

> This passage recounts the Lord's words to Israel before they crossed the Jordan into the promised land. The Lord promised not to abandon or destroy His people. What did He also promise not to forget (v. 31)?

At the beginning of our study, we looked at the covenant God made with Abraham for all of Israel and her descendants (see pp. 14–15). Deuteronomy 4:31 references that covenant, one that God would keep even when His people had been driven into faraway places. I can't help but imagine that Mordecai knew enough about passages like Deuteronomy 4 to know that God would not fail the Jewish people now. Even though Mordecai and his people were seemingly a million miles from the land of promise, Esther was queen in a pagan Persian palace, and Mordecai had angered a chief rival of the Jews by not bowing down to him, somehow, someway, God would keep His promise to preserve His beloved people.

Personal Response: In what area of your life is God asking you to live according to His promises—even if you don't know how it's all going to work out?

Mordecai believed that God *would* work out deliverance, but he didn't know *how*. When it comes to significant outcomes in my life, I very much like to know both the "will" and the "how." But it's precisely the latter that God doesn't usually share with me. He delights in our trusting Him, even when we don't know the specifics of the ways in which He will work out His plans. Let's look at a few encouraging verses that speak to these situations in our lives.

Trust in the Lord with all your heart, and do not rely on your own understanding; in all your ways know him, and he will make your paths straight.

PROVERBS 3:5-6

How do these verses encourage you to trust the Lord with your life's direction?

Humble yourselves, therefore, under the mighty hand of God, so that he may exalt you at the proper time, casting all your cares on him, because he cares about you.

1 PETER 5:6-7

We don't have to stuff or ignore our cares. Instead, what are we to do with them, and why?

Esther and Mordecai had the confidence to courageously step up, not because God told them how things would turn out, or that their lives would be spared, but because they knew that fighting for the Jewish people was in accordance with His will.

Personal Reflection: Earlier you were asked to describe an area in your life where you're not sure which way to go, or which option to choose. What do you know about the general will of God that can help inform your decision?

Esther and Mordecai didn't have a step-by-step plan from God; rather, they knew what was true about Him, and they made a plan according to that knowledge. What is your next right step?

Romans 8:28 says, "And we know that in all things God works for the good of those who love him, who have been called according to his purpose" (NIV). Many things in life are not good. And bad things don't always work together for good. However, what we can bank on is that in *all things* it is *God* who is working for our good![8]

Be obedient to Christ. Make choices according to what God has revealed to you in His Word. Trust Him. Though you can't know how it's all going to work out, take heart that it will. In His time, in His way, always for your good.

Fasting *on the* Way *to* Feasting

ESTHER 4:15-17

Today we reach an important transition in Esther's character. We will witness her moving from a place of dependence to one of taking charge. She will now give righteous orders, fast for God's deliverance, and risk her life in obedience. In light of these details, I was surprised to read one Jewish scholar's take on Esther. Michael Fox wrote, "Her very ordinariness suggests that ordinary people too can rise to the moment and take on unexpected strength."[9]

Ordinary?

That's not the first word that comes to mind when I think of Esther. You know, with her exceptional beauty, palace life, and that one small tidbit about her being QUEEN. But after further reflection, I found myself resonating with this scholar's assessment. Watch how Esther begins to step into her God-given position and authority. Notice the ways she goes from "ordinary" to exceptionally courageous.

READ ESTHER 4:13-17.

What did Esther command Mordecai to do?

What did Esther also commit to doing, along with her female servants?

What did Esther say she would do after the three-day fast, even if it was against the law?

How did Mordecai respond to Esther's commands?

Personal Take: It's noteworthy that Esther chose to fast along with Mordecai and the rest of the Jews. She could have ordered them to fast while she enjoyed the delicacies of the palace. What do her actions tell you about her character, identity with the Jews, and her role as a servant leader?

Fasting contrasts with feasting in the book of Esther. While the Persian empire threw lavish banquets, God's people humbled themselves by forgoing food and drink. Interestingly, fasting is mentioned more frequently in the post-exilic era than it is before the exile. After the destruction of the temple, it seems the Jews had a renewed desperation and earnest need for God.[10]

Personal Reflection: How has the Lord used lean times to deepen your relationship with Him, perhaps even more than celebratory ones?

It's implied that Esther's call for a nation-wide fast was an appeal for God to do the miraculous and give her favor with King Ahasuerus.[11] Once again, prayer is not specifically mentioned, but in keeping with Israel's history, fasting and prayer went together. We learn from the prophet Isaiah that while fasting is a productive practice, it's important that we fast the way God intends.

READ ISAIAH 58.

Soak this chapter in. It's filled with restorative imagery and calls us from a life of cold religiosity to active kingdom building.

Why did God not respond to the Israelites' fasting (vv. 3-4,9)?

What had they ignored that was important to God's heart (vv. 6-7,10)?

How many times have we tried to manipulate God by giving a tithe, praying a prayer, or not missing church, all the while disregarding His commands to take care of the poor, look after our family members, stop gossiping, or live morally pure lives? This passage is deeply convicting to me.

> Personal Reflection: After reading Isaiah 58, what aspects of God's commands might you be overlooking? I'll share my reflection with you to get you started. *Not ignoring the needs of our family members stood out to me in verse 7. The Lord wants me to serve my own "flesh and blood" from my heart. Oftentimes, serving our family members goes unnoticed or unappreciated. But what a great reminder it is that the way we take care of our family is dear to God's heart.* Now, it's your turn.

NOW TURN TO MATTHEW AND READ VERSES 6:16-18.

Fasting is a way of humbling ourselves before the Lord, not a means of manipulating Him to do our bidding. It's also not a way to receive pats on the back—we know we're not in the right spiritual frame of mind if we fast so people will applaud us and tell us how holy we are for skipping the waffles and fried chicken at lunch. Fasting is a special discipline, but we must practice it with sincere hearts.

> **LOOK BACK AT ESTHER 4:16.** FILL IN THE BLANK: Esther decided she would approach the king *before* or *after* the fast? _____

Sometimes, we fast for direction. We're not sure which way to go, what job to take, or what move to make, so we fast and pray for God's guidance. Other times, we know exactly what God wants us to do, and we fast for His favor as we walk out our obedience. Esther's fast falls into the second category. She had already made up her mind that she would go to the king and seek his favor on behalf of her people. Confident in her decision, she and the community fell before the Lord in humility, pleading for His help.

TRUE OR FALSE? Esther knew beyond a shadow of a doubt that God would rescue her and her people from genocide.

FILL IN THE BLANK: After Esther gave her orders, she said, "If I perish, I _____."

Esther didn't treat the fast as a bargaining chip. Instead, she confidently left the results with Almighty God, come what may.

You may be walking through a situation where a job is on the line, a loved one's health is waning, or a divorce is tearing apart family members. Our knee-jerk reaction is to tell God what He needs to do, how He needs to do it, and the timeline He needs to do it in—because we always have a timeline. But Esther's statement, "If I perish, I perish"—even if extreme when compared to most of our circumstances—is a wonderful reminder that we can trust God with the outcome.

Personal Response: Is there a situation or relationship in your life where prayer and fasting are needed? If you're new to fasting, are you willing to skip a meal and use that time for dedicated prayer? If you've fasted before, are you willing to do it again, perhaps fasting over the course of the day? Respond by writing about the situation and a plan to fast and pray, if fasting is safe for you to do. (Refer to the next page for a few additional thoughts about fasting.)

Dear friend, our God is good. He is faithful. He is sovereign. He rules the universe. He paid our ransom. He gave us His Holy Spirit to guide and encourage us. Come before Him today and bring your concerns and burdens into His compassionate care.

Fasting

Fasting is an important activity in the book of Esther. It is one of the few practices mentioned that was a well-documented part of Israel's life pre-exile. Below are five principles about fasting, excerpted from my Bible study, *Encountering God*.

1. Fasting is not a way to manipulate God to do what you want Him to do (Isa. 58). When we fast we're voluntarily putting ourselves in a place of weakness and dependence upon God, trusting Him with the results of our fast.

2. When we fast we're forgoing something natural in pursuit of the supernatural. Jesus feasted on bread that was not of this world. Fasting has helped me become more aware of the spiritual realm that is often obscured by my earthly yearnings.

3. When we fast we're practicing the needed discipline of saying "no" to ourselves and "yes" to God. In a culture that prizes the ideas of on-demand, you deserve it, don't go without, we desperately need to tell ourselves "no" on occasion. While this may seem inhibiting at first, it's paradoxically liberating. When I have control over my body, when I'm not "hangry" several times a week, when my temperament isn't ruled by my next meal, there is freedom.

Fasting puts life in perspective and aligns our hearts with the Lord's.

4. Fasting is a great way of taking the focus off myself and placing it on God and others. When all I want is a piece of pizza there's something good and powerful about interceding for those who may not have eaten for days, for those suffering in our community and abroad, for the specific needs only God can meet. Fasting puts life in perspective and aligns our hearts with the Lord's.

5. Fasting teaches me contentment. When my body isn't immediately satisfied, or life deals me a series of disappointments, fasting helps me practice the habit of going to the Lord and seeking satisfaction from Him instead of what is readily available to me. (Like my prized stash of dark chocolate peanut butter cups that solve a multitude of ailments.)

Fasting is worth it, my dear friends. I pray you will incorporate it into your semi-regular rhythm of life. . . . Gather with others to pray during your fasting. Plan times to be with the Lord or with others in fellowship. And most of all, feast.[12]

From Ordinary to Extraordinary

ESTHER 5:1-8

Growing up in the church, I was exposed to many great Old Testament names of the faith. From Noah to Abraham, Ruth, Hannah, Samuel, Deborah, David, Daniel, Nehemiah, and Esther—heroes abound. But so do the flawed in the faith, sometimes even the failed in the faith. What I don't remember hearing so often is that the heroes of the faith are *the same people* as the flawed and failed.

This doesn't mean we should plan for a life of mediocre faith, setting the bar low because most everyone in the Old Testament had some really shaky moments. If we take that approach, we miss the presence of the Holy Spirit who enables us to live lives of remarkable goodness (Eph. 2:10)! At the same time, since we're all aware of our human frailty, we can take great comfort that God called a once obscure Esther to a moment of defining faith. We can't forget that Queen Esther who saved the Jews is the same Esther who was once an unknown orphan and exile, living more like a Persian than a Torah-abiding Jew. I believe Michael Fox is correct. Esther's ordinariness *is* a testament that ordinary people can turn extraordinary when they step out in obedient faith.[13]

I'm excited to watch Esther step into her God-given role as queen while simultaneously owning her identity as one of God's people.

READ ESTHER 4:15-17 AND 5:1.

On what day of the fast did Esther approach the palace?

What action steps did Esther take after fasting? List each one she took.

Personal Reflection: The apostle James says that we demonstrate our faith by our works (Jas. 2:18). He puts it even more bluntly when he says that faith without works is dead (Jas. 2:20). How do Esther's actions reveal her faith?

One of the actions Esther took was putting on her royal clothes. The Hebrew word for "royal clothing" is *malkut*, and it literally means *royalty*. In other words, Esther woke up, got up, and *put on royalty*.[14] That will preach! Up to this point, Esther's position as queen did not amount to much more than a title. Now, however, she began to wear her identity, to walk in and leverage it—not for her own glory, but for the sake of God's people.

Personal Take: After three days of fasting, Esther must have been in a state of physical weakness. Why do you think she would approach the most important day of her life physically weak instead of strong?

LOOK BACK AT 4:12. How long had it been since Esther had been asked to approach the king?

Personal Take: Imagine if you were one of the Jews participating in Esther's fast. What would you be praying for? (Think beyond the prayer that God would save you.)

I have to imagine that Esther, Mordecai, and the rest of the Jews were praying that the king would summon Esther. Why? Because Esther could only safely approach King Ahasuerus if he requested her presence. What's more, she had not been summoned in thirty days. If she approached him uninvited, she would be executed—unless he extended his golden scepter toward her. That *unless* would have been one of my prayers!

For three days, no word from the palace came. Surely, the silence would be broken at any moment, the Jews must have thought. A thunderous knock on the door requesting her majesty's presence was bound to happen any second now. God would answer them, right? (At least this is how I imagine it.)

But after three days of fasting, nothing. Only silence. Perhaps the palace was preoccupied by other business, or the king with other women. Heaven must have felt terribly distant. Had God stopped hearing their prayers? Would He rescue them all the way in Persia?

Personal Response: At the end of the three-day fast, Esther put on her royal clothes and proceeded to the palace, despite not being summoned. How does her courageous step of faith encourage you?

READ ESTHER 5:2-8.

When the king saw Esther facing the palace, he had both an internal and external reaction (v. 2). What were they?

1. The king's internal reaction:

2. The king's external reaction:

The king may not have summoned Esther, but he extended to her his golden scepter, and that was all she needed. For now. Esther gained favor like she had many times before (2:9,15,17; 5:2). God's providence is all over this scene. And a woman's obedience married to God's providence is a powerful thing.

After the king asked Esther what she wanted, and after he agreed to go above and beyond her request, Esther responded by inviting him and Haman to a banquet.

Personal Take: What surprises you about Esther's request? What do you think she was trying to accomplish?

Ahasuerus reacted with urgency, commanding his subordinates to summon Haman. They arrived at Esther's banquet on time. We can't miss the providential parallel between Esther 1:10-12 and 5:4-5.

Compare and contrast both passages below.

	ESTHER 1:10-12	ESTHER 5:4-5
WHO INVITES WHOM?		
THE RESPONSES		
THE SETTING		

In the beginning of the story, the king commanded Queen Vashti to come to his banquet and she refused. Today, Esther invites the king to her banquet and he accepts. At this point in the story, power is being transferred Esther's way. Maybe not formally or legally, but practically.

REREAD ESTHER 5:6-8.

Imagine the setting. Listen to the sounds of a lavish feast. The generous pours of wine into goblets echoing across the room. Conversation flowing as freely as the drinks. Esther choosing her words carefully, waiting for her moment. Ahasuerus finally asking what it is exactly that Esther wants.

We, the audience, hold our breath. We're ready for Esther to reveal her identity, to explain the nature of the edict Haman has put in place, to ask for the whole thing to be overturned. But instead, with the longest drumroll in the history of the world sounding in the background, Esther delays her request and asks if the king and Haman will return the next day for a second banquet.

Twice the king asked what Esther wanted. Twice he offered to exceed her desires. Twice Esther made interim requests while delaying her true one. The question is, *Why?* Was she fearful? Nervous? Procrastinating? Calculating?

Personal Take: Why do you think Esther delayed putting forth her request? Support your reasoning.

I tend to think Esther was planning and maneuvering here. In keeping with the strength and resolve she was displaying, it appears she was taking decisive steps, even if she was unsure how her plan would work out. But what's important for us to recognize is not how assertive or scared, purposeful or procrastinating, brilliant or bumbling Esther proved to be at the banquet table. What we must see is that Almighty God was working all things out according to His covenant promise with His people. No matter Esther's disposition, God is fully in control.

Personal Reflection: How does God's providence in the book of Esther encourage you in a specific situation where an outcome is currently out of your control?

We will have to wait a little longer to study the moment Esther made her request known. Since you have already read the story, you know that a whole lot of drama happens between banquet number one and banquet number two. In the meantime, ponder this fascinating detail: Esther is referred to as Queen Esther fourteen times in the story, thirteen of which come *after* verse 5:1.[15] Scholar Leland Ryken writes that Esther, who is initially known for her youth and beauty, is "transformed into a person with heroic moral stature and political skill."[16]

Once Esther identifies with God's people, she steps into her true position as queen.

My goodness, there is so much for us to receive from this insight. As believers in Jesus, how often do we take for granted our identity in Christ? How often do we leave the virtues of the Spirit hanging in our closets unworn and unappreciated? How much easier is it to find our worth in our accomplishments, rather than in the One who bought us by His blood? Are you laying aside your identity in Christ for what the surrounding culture celebrates?

GOSPEL MOMENT

READ REVELATION 19:6-8. As the bride of Christ, what are we given to wear?

You and I can "put on royalty" because of who we are in Christ. We can stand and face the daunting palace of power, not because we're unafraid, but because we know whose we are. We can leave the condemnation from our past behind and step into robes of righteousness because we've been given them freely. We can sit down at a banquet with foes because we know God is sovereign over our affairs.

Personal Response: Picture yourself as God sees you—clothed in the righteousness of Christ (Gal. 3:27). In what way is God asking you to step into your God-given identity as His beloved child?

Creamy Sun-Dried Tomato Pasta

This is my new pasta go-to. Your family and friends will think you went to more work than you did and the heavy cream will make them think you're a better cook than you are. Plus, this dish reheats nicely.

INGREDIENTS

- 1 (8 oz) jar oil-packed sun-dried tomatoes
- 1 lb. boneless skinless chicken breasts, cubed
- 4 tsp Italian seasoning
- 1 tsp paprika
- Pinch red pepper flakes
- Salt & pepper to taste
- 3/4 cup grated parmesan cheese

- 2 Tbs salted butter
- 1 medium shallot
- 3 cloves garlic, chopped
- 1 lb. rigatoni
- 1 cup heavy cream
- 3 tsp Dijon mustard
- 2 cups baby spinach (remove stems if present)
- Wedge of lemon juice per plate

DIRECTIONS

1. Pour 3 tablespoons of oil from sun-dried tomato jar into a large pot. (I use my Dutch oven.) Set sun-dried tomatoes aside, chop if you want smaller pieces.

2. Set pot over medium-high heat. Add chicken, 3 teaspoons of Italian seasoning, paprika, and a pinch of red pepper flakes, salt, and pepper. Cook until golden brown, about 5-7 minutes. Add ¼ cup parmesan, stir for about a minute, remove the chicken from pot and set aside.

3. To the same pot, add butter, shallot, garlic, and remaining teaspoon of Italian seasoning. Saute until fragrant, about 3 minutes. Add 3 ½ cups water. Bring to a boil, add rigatoni and stir often until pasta is al dente, 8 minutes. Stir in heavy cream, mustard, remaining ½ cup parmesan, spinach, and chopped sun-dried tomatoes. Add set-aside chicken and any juices back into pot. To serve top with squeezed lemon juice and fresh parmesan.[17]

Watch the Session Four Video

Use the space below to follow along with the outline points from Kelly's teaching. A leader guide is available for free download at **lifeway.com/estherstudy**.

1. God will accomplish _____ one way or

another; it's up to us if we want to _____.

2. When Esther decides to _____ herself with God's

covenant and His people, she begins to _____!

3. Esther knew enough about _____ to

make a _____.

4. God _____ for Esther but not before

she _____.

To access the video sessions, use the instructions
in the back of your Bible study book.

In Between
Two
Banquets

I Can't Get No Satisfaction

ESTHER 5:9-14

We pick our story back up in that frustrating spot we all know too well—waiting, while in the dark about what lies ahead. We don't like to wait, especially when we don't know how things will turn out. But this is where we find Esther, bless her. After a chess match of a banquet, I imagine her crawling into her queen bed (I can't help it when these puns write themselves), where she tossed and turned all night, playing in her head every possible outcome of tomorrow's meeting.

She was in between two banquets.

The first went fine, but the second had to rival the most-successful-banquet-of-her-life, as the future of an entire people group hung on their conversation.

Interestingly, the narrative momentarily leaves Esther and focuses its attention on Haman and the king. But we don't want to forget that, while we are kept abreast of everything happening at Haman's house and in the king's bedroom, Esther was in the dark. We will share God's vantage point of knowing and seeing everything, but only long enough to be encouraged and reminded that even when we can't see what God is up to, He is always at work.

READ ESTHER 5:9-14.

What is concerning about Haman's swing of emotions in verse 9?

What made Haman content and happy?

On the other hand, what made Haman dissatisfied and angry?

Haman seemingly had it all, yet Mordecai's rejection sent him reeling. Although extreme, some aspects of Haman's emotions feel familiar. Like my friend Brooke pointed out, we often tend to fixate on the negative, even if we get a ton of positive feedback.

Personal Take: LOOK MORE CLOSELY AT VERSES 11-13.

What do you think Haman sought from his wife and friends?

What do you think was the reason for Haman's emotional instability?

A person like Haman is our worst nightmare. When he visited with his wife and friends, he talked only about himself. In fact, that was the entire point of the gathering—a forum where he could prattle on about his accomplishments while his audience was forced to listen. I doubt he asked anyone else how their day was or how they were doing. This is to be expected because his emotions were not his own. He was a slave to the reactions of others. If people revered and applauded him, his spirits soared. If he was on the short list of invitations, he felt important. To be powerful was to matter. But Haman was a party balloon that could be punctured at any moment. In went the pin of Mordecai's rejection, and out zipped Haman's self-worth.

Personal Reflection: Do you find yourself significantly rising or falling on the approval of others? If so, describe what the ups and downs look like.

Haman had an idolatry problem. He worshiped power, prestige, and pleasure. He was upbeat when these gods were working for him. When they weren't, he crumbled into a desperate heap. I wrote a Bible study on the topic of idolatry called *No Other Gods: The Unrivaled Pursuit of Christ*. I share this because idolatry is not foreign to me. While Haman is an extreme version of our worst selves, his pride, selfishness, and insecurities are familiar to us all. Consider just one example of this—social media. How often do we post to genuinely share with and encourage others, versus posting for affirmation or a sense of accomplishment? Idolatry can be subtle.

But there is hope! I want you to be encouraged today. But to get there, we have to investigate what may be causing some of our own emotional highs and lows.

READ 1 JOHN 2:15-17.

How does John define "loving the world" in verse 16?

Why is it unwise to love the sinful things of the world?

What is the blessing for those who do the will of the Father?

John's use of "the world" here is not referring to the delights we experience on earth, rather the ungodly pull of systems that are at odds with God's glory and good will. It is fitting that we relish the many blessings and good gifts God has given us to enjoy. This is quite different from being consumed by hedonistic pleasures that not only stoke our pride but always leave us longing for more.

READ JAMES 4:1-3.

Sometimes we find ourselves angry, arguing with others, or chronically dissatisfied because we're not asking God for what we need. And when we do ask, we ask with selfish motives.

Personal Reflection: What challenges you about the 1 John and James passages?

NOW READ JAMES 4:6-10.

James offers an antidote to a life of internal unrest. We don't have to live in a state of insecurity, jealousy, or striving to be the best in the room.

Personal Response: How can you humble yourself, resist the devil, and draw near to Jesus today? Be specific in your answer as you reflect on lessons learned from Haman's emotions and actions.

Power, success, money, fame, the applause of people—it's a mere pile of kindling. It flashes with promising flame, but before we know it, we're left warming ourselves by embers. The late Matthew Perry wrote, "I was a guy who wanted to become famous. There was steam coming out of my ears, I wanted to be famous so badly. You want the attention, you want the bucks, and you want the best seat in the restaurant. I didn't think what the repercussions would be. . . . Now all these years later, I'm certain that I got famous so I would not waste my entire life trying to get famous. You have to get famous to know that it's not the answer. And nobody who is not famous will ever truly believe that."[1]

Except, we can believe it in faith. The abiding testimony of Scripture is that our happiness, worth, and contentment are bound up in our relationship with Christ, not in our stuff or accomplishments (Luke 12:15; 11:43). It wouldn't have helped Haman to try to walk away from the pursuit of being number one. He needed God to be first in his life. That's the only way to dethrone an idol in our lives. This has never changed.

GOSPEL MOMENT

Jesus says in Matthew 6:33, "But seek first the kingdom of God and his righteousness, and all these things will be provided for you." Pray that you will live today seeking Jesus's fame and renown. Pray that you will run after His righteousness no matter what else you may have to leave behind. He is everything.

Who Are You Listening to?

ESTHER 5:14

Who we surround ourselves with is one of the most defining ingredients of our lives. We live and breathe not just as individuals but as parts of families, friendship circles, churches, groups, and communities. Since it's hard not to become like those we spend time with, it's important we choose our friends wisely. My closest community is never hesitant to remind me to die to my selfish desires, take the high road, choose love, be prayerful, and make decisions that bring God glory. These are the underpinnings of their lives and they help shape my own.

Two days ago, my friend Mary Katharine told me I needed to trust God with something I was trying to manage myself. It rankled me every which way. But here I am, two days later, the better for her counsel. If we're around godly people, it does more than rub off—it sinks in. And the reverse is just as true. We are influenced by the words and countenances of others, and with that indefinable aura they bring into the room. Are you around those who display the fruit of the Spirit (Gal. 5:22-23) or those who spread the fumes of their selfish actions (Gal. 5:16-21)? As we'll see today, our closest companions shape the people we are and will become, for better or worse.

READ ESTHER 5:9-14,
REPEATED FROM YESTERDAY'S READING.

What kept Haman from finding satisfaction in his other accomplishments (v. 13)?

Personal Reflection: Think about when a spouse, child, or loved one is chronically dissatisfied. What burden does it place on you? How do you respond?

What advice did Haman's wife, Zeresh, and his friends give Haman in order to assuage his anger and despair?

REFLECT ON THE FOLLOWING PROVERBS and answer the corresponding questions.

Pride comes before destruction,
and an arrogant spirit before a fall.

PROVERBS 16:18

How is this a warning for someone like Haman?

A violent person lures his neighbor,
leading him on a path that is not good.

PROVERBS 16:29

How does this describe Zeresh and Haman's friends?

Everyone with a proud heart is detestable to the Lord;
be assured, he will not go unpunished.

PROVERBS 16:5

What is "detestable to the Lᴏʀᴅ"?

An angry person stirs up conflict,
and a hot-tempered one increases rebellion.

PROVERBS 29:22

How was conflict stirred up and rebellion increased in Esther 5:14?

Esther 5:9-14 is a perfect example of someone giving bad advice to someone with a bad attitude. Before we think that Haman and Zeresh are the only ones who do this kind of thing, we should realize that we do this too. A friend gets hurt by someone, and to help her get even we tell her how high she should build the metaphorical gallows. Whether we're on the receiving end of advice that stirs our anger or giving that kind of advice, Scripture offers us a better way. Consider the example of Abigail from 1 Samuel.

First, some context: Abigail was a wise and able woman married to a wicked and violent man named Nabal (1 Sam. 25). King David sent servants to Nabal to ask for provisions for his men. Prior to his request, David had treated Nabal's servants well and expected to be treated with equal kindness. Nabal not only refused to give provision to David's men but he mocked David in the process. David didn't love this, to say the least. He instructed four hundred of his men to strap on their swords and wipe out Nabal, his family, and servants. When Abigail heard about David's plot, she mounted her donkey with a load of gifts, but more importantly, with a load of life-saving counsel.

READ 1 SAMUEL 25:23-39.

> What character traits does Abigail possess? How does she contrast with Zeresh?

Abigail doesn't just give good advice, she gives godly advice.

> In what meaningful and moving ways does Abigail remind David of who the Lord is and how He acts toward His people? Briefly compile what she says about Him.

Personal Reflection: What part of Abigail's counsel stands out as most meaningful to you in your current circumstances and why?

When David heard that Nabal was dead, he blessed God for championing his cause and for restraining him from evil. God used Abigail to hold David back from irreversible consequences. What a gorgeous description of the power of godly counsel, which restrains us from doing what we are sure to regret, and compels us toward mercy, grace, and trust in God's matchless sovereignty to accomplish His purposes. Zeresh and Haman's advisors counseled him in the opposite direction. "Show no restraint!" they exclaimed. "Build the gallows as high as you can!" they chanted. "Eliminate your enemy, so you can be happy!" We'll see how this turned out for Haman tomorrow.

Personal Reflection: Let's reflect on two sides of the same coin.

On the one side, how well do you receive wise counsel? What is your immediate reaction when confronted with hard but necessary truth?

On the other side, what kind of counsel are you most apt to give— what a loved one wants to hear, or what they need to hear?

Proverbs 15:31-33 says, "One who listens to life-giving rebukes will be at home among the wise. Anyone who ignores discipline despises himself, but whoever listens to correction acquires good sense." We may think we want friends who tell us to build death traps for those who wound us, but what we need are life-giving rebukes when we're headed in the wrong direction. We need people who will tell us the truth about God, ourselves, and the world.

Personal Response:

How can you give better advice today that is in keeping with love and truth?

How can you receive godly counsel today, perhaps counsel you've been resisting?

It's easy to miss the practical implications of Esther 5:14 because of how extreme it is. But most of us can agree it's also easy to encourage loved ones toward seeking revenge or nursing bitterness. We don't want to be accomplices in another person's sin by stirring up division. We want to be champions of healing and wholeness. This doesn't mean we cover our eyes to injustice or ignore wrong doing. It means we encourage with the truths of Scripture, we direct one another to Jesus, and we trust that God is able to mete out vengeance and justice in His time (Heb. 10:30-31).

When You Can't Sleep

ESTHER 6:1-3

Sleeping used to be my secret power. It didn't matter what time I went to bed, I could sleep. If a nap was an option, I was a seasoned and eager participant. Jet lag was no match for my capabilities. People who couldn't fall asleep or stay asleep were enigmas to me. What was so challenging about literally laying down and tuning out for eight hours? Then I turned forty-seven.

I cannot begin to explain the biological science to you, all I know is I am now conscious between the hours of one and three in the morning, and it is torture. In my best moments, I pray. In my acceptable ones, I think. In the most desperate of times, I play Wordle®. What I have never done, purely for logistical reasons, is ask one of my servants to read me the royal chronicles of palace business so I can fall back asleep. In case you're wondering what life might be like if such light and interesting reading were available to you, we're about to find out.

Personal Reflection: To get us into the spirit of today's study, have you ever had a moment of clarification or a spiritually meaningful experience in the middle of a sleepless night? If so, describe what happened.

READ ESTHER 6:1-3. What did Ahasuerus discover (or remember) about Mordecai in the official written report?

REREAD ESTHER 2:21-23 and paraphrase the details of the event to refresh your memory.

NOW RETURN TO CHAPTER 6. When the king asked his attendants what honor and recognition had been given to Mordecai, what was their response (v. 3)?

The CSB translation of 6:3 reads, "*Nothing* has been done for him" (emphasis mine). Five years had passed since Mordecai foiled Bigthana and Teresh's plot to assassinate the king. Not only was nothing done for Mordecai, but his archenemy Haman had risen to prominence and was behind a decree to destroy Mordecai and his people. Whatever happened to good things happening to good people?

Personal Reflection: Think of a time when you stuck your neck out, sacrificed, or went the extra mile for someone and "nothing" was done for you. Perhaps you weren't recognized, or even thanked. How did you get through this? If with the Lord's help, be specific about how He helped you.

We all experience being overlooked. At some point we will be passed over for a promotion we deserve. A role or position we worked for will go to a person with little integrity. We will sacrifice significantly for someone we love, only for that person to be enamored with someone else for lesser reasons. The injustice can be frustrating and even heartbreaking. Thankfully, Scripture comforts us and reframes our perspective. Like Mordecai, we can't stop doing the right thing just because we aren't acknowledged or rewarded. This is in part because, as believers, we work for something truer, better, and higher than another person's favor.

READ HEBREWS 6:10-12. The author of Hebrews says that God is not . . .

Unkind   Unjust   Unrewarding   Uncharitable

What will God not forget?

Personal Reflection: How do these truths encourage you when someone isn't giving you what you deserve or hope for?

READ GALATIANS 6:7-10.

What does Paul tell us about the nature of sowing and reaping?

Why does he tell us not to tire of doing what is good and right?

It's natural to desire recognition when we've helped someone or done something worthy of reward. A well-earned acknowledgment is a worthy affirmation that rightly encourages us. Simultaneously, reward and affirmation from others will never convince us we're enough. People were never meant to fully satisfy our sense of self-worth. Only when God commends us is it enough.

Before returning to Esther, I want to look at a few more passages in the New Testament. If God's glory and His reward are the true longings of our heart, then we will no longer live and die by acknowledgment from others (2 Cor. 10:17-18).

READ MATTHEW 6:1-4 AND 6:16-18. What does Jesus tell us about how the Father responds to those who give and fast for the right reasons?

READ JOHN 12:42-43. What did the Jewish leaders desire more than praise from God?

READ JOHN 5:44. The religious leaders accepted glory from

_____, but didn't seek it from _____.

Contrary to our instincts, seeking God's rewards isn't selfish, it's a matter of trust. Because God promises to reward us when we glorify Him through obedience, we show that we trust Him when we believe He will reward us—because that's what He says He will do!

It was common practice for Persian kings to publicly reward those who were courageous and loyal as a way of promoting the king's safety in dangerous times.[2] That Mordecai had gone unrewarded for his loyalty to the king was an oversight, to say the least. "His willingness to overlook the slight and continue faithfully to serve the king gives insight into his character."[3]

Personal Reflection: How does God's faithfulness to Mordecai concretely encourage you in whatever season you're in?

Proverbs 21:1 says, "A king's heart is like channeled water in the Lord's hand: He directs it wherever he chooses."

What is God's relationship to kings or world leaders?

Ahasuerus's sleepless night led him to ask for the court records, which led him to remember Mordecai's selfless acts, which resulted in him wanting to honor Mordecai. What appears to be an ordinary chain of events was nothing less than God's providential hand in action. The heart of a pagan king is not beyond God's ability to direct it wherever He will.

Personal Prayer: What are you trying to control? Take time to place it in God's hands, confessing that He is more than able to handle whatever you're facing.

The king may have forgotten to honor Mordecai, but God had not. Be encouraged. The same God who didn't forget His people then won't forget you now. Seek Him for the reward that only He can give. And make no mistake, He Himself is your greatest reward.

Between Banquets

ESTHER 6:4-10

We are still in the middle of Esther's two banquets, where the fate of Esther, Mordecai, and the Jews is far from settled. The king can't sleep, his servants are reading to him from the official court records, and Haman is approaching the court after having erected gallows for Mordecai. The palace is abuzz, but the two main characters, Esther and Mordecai, are elsewhere. They are presumably trying to sleep while the weight of the world presses against their chests. That Esther and Mordecai have no immediate part in this height of intrigue is significant. It tells us something about God's sovereignty. It tells us something about ourselves. We'll discover more about each in today's study.

READ ESTHER 6:1-10.

From yesterday's reading, what led to the king realizing Mordecai had gone without being honored?

Who "just so happened" to walk into the king's outer court the moment the king realized his oversight of Mordecai?

Esther   Bigthana   Mordecai   Haman

Why was Haman at the king's court so early in the morning (v. 4)?

List everything Haman suggests the king should do for the person he wants to honor (vv. 8-9). If you're a more visual learner, sketch a picture of what Haman describes in the box below.

Haman thought he was planning his own ceremony of honor when detailing his vision to the king. You may have expected him to ask for more money, or perhaps a promotion. But Haman already had all the wealth a person could reasonably enjoy, and he was second only to the king in authority.

Personal Take: What do you imagine Haman thought he could gain, that he didn't already have, by wearing the royal robes of the king and riding on his horse through the city square?

I recently saw a picture on social media of a global superstar wearing the jacket of her celebrity boyfriend to an after party. Socials were abuzz. A mere piece of fabric, in this instance the jacket, symbolized their relationship status. It told the world that she was with him, and he was with her. Apparently, wearing someone else's jacket, or royal robe, has been a thing for a few thousand years.

READ 1 SAMUEL 18:1-5.

This scene takes place prior to the Persian period, at the beginning of Israel's monarchy. Saul was king and his son Jonathan was heir to the throne.

How did Jonathan symbolize his covenant with David (v. 4)?

Whatever actual power was transferred to David the day Jonathan put his robes on him is uncertain. What is apparent, however, is the authority and royalty that the king's robes foreshadowed. We'll revisit this concept tomorrow.

LOOK BACK AT ESTHER 6:10. Given the significance of wearing a king (or future king's) robes, what might this verse forecast about Mordecai's future?

You can argue that verse 10 is the hinge on which the whole story swings the other direction. Up until this moment the narrative has driven toward catastrophe—the bad guys prospering and the good guys languishing and being passed over. But God has never lost control of the story. He has never failed to keep His covenant promises with Israel, even though the Jews lay scattered across the Persian empire due to their forefather's disobedience. The gallows Haman built for Mordecai would ultimately be Haman's own demise, and the honor he planned for himself would propel Mordecai's rise to power. How about that for a divine reversal? How about that for God's sovereignty?

My own simple definition of God's sovereignty is:

God's rule and reign over every part of His creation, in particular in the lives of His people, to bring about His ultimate will in all things.

Personal Take: What stands out most to you about the evidence of God's sovereignty in today's passage?

Sometimes, we have to start at the end and work backwards to see what God was doing at a time when His sovereignty was not all that obvious to us. Esther 6 drips with irony, but it's only visible in hindsight. Haman "just so happened" to be in the court the moment the king realized that Mordecai had gone unrewarded. Haman's "chance" arrival came right at the time the king was mulling over Mordecai's reward. Haman ironically planned his own moment of honor, only to discover he was actually planning Mordecai's!

This scene is brought to you by the mundane and ordinary detail of a sleepless night. Or is it? I think we can all agree that God's hand is quite obviously moving on behalf of His people. He is able to use sleeplessness, selfishness, forgetfulness, and folly to accomplish His will—nothing is too lowly or lofty when it comes to what He will employ for His purposes. My friend Haley said it best, "God may not be mentioned in this book, but He's all over it!"

That Esther and Mordecai aren't direct participants in this turn of events might be my favorite part of the story. In a sense, God does His best work when both of them are absent. This doesn't take anything away from their astounding courage and obedience, but it gives all glory to God.

Personal Reflection: What does this part of Esther's story tell you about God's sovereign activity in your life, even when you're absent or powerless to affect your situation?

The times I feel most out of control are the times when I am just that—without control. I feel much better when I can effect change by my decisions, resources, and connections. I feel most vulnerable when I'm at the mercy of someone else. Whether we're under the knife of a surgeon, waiting on a boss to promote us, hoping a lawyer will take up our case, or beholden to the decisions of a spouse, waiting and powerlessness seem to go hand in hand. But here's the reality: If our lives are bound up in Christ's, and our future is in God's hands, no circumstance is ever truly in or out of our control—God governs it all.

Personal Response: What area of your life feels out of control? How are you comforted by God's activity in Ahasuerus's palace even in Esther and Mordecai's absence?

God is able to reverse fortunes and destinies on a dime, and sometimes He does just that. When I was in my twenties, I rented a room from a single woman in her mid-thirties. She wanted to be married, have children, and change career paths. Within a few months, she met the love of her life, sold her house for a fortune (the one I was living in), got married, got pregnant, and quit her job. It was the fastest turn of events I'd ever witnessed in a person's life, and, yes, I had to find a new place to live, which is beside the point (but was very much the point for me at the time).

We can expect that God will continue to transform our lives, but we can't presume to know how. We may or may not be able to get pregnant, find a spouse, save a marriage, make the mortgage payment, get promoted, or be physically healed. Oh, but don't think this means you're destined for second best.

God rescues the lowly from the ash heap, He puts the orphans in families, He supplies wine and grain on tables that once had only crumbs. We can say along with Jacob that we went out with just our staff but have returned with family, friends, and flocks (Gen. 32:10)!

READ 1 PETER 5:6-7,

Humble yourselves, therefore, under the mighty hand of God, so that he may exalt you at the proper time, casting all your cares on him, because he cares about you.

Why does the Lord tell us to cast our cares on Him?

How is humility tied into this command?

The Lord has your future, He has your circumstances, and He has you. You can give Him your burdens and anxiety because He cares deeply for you. Even when you are most powerless to affect the outcome of your current situation—like Esther and Mordecai—He is at work.

As the late C. H. Spurgeon is quoted to have said, "When you go through a trial, the sovereignty of God is the pillow upon which you lay your head."[4] He works even in the middle of the night.

The End of the Wicked

ESTHER 6:11-14

Why do the wicked prosper?

Or, in modern and broader language, why do the undeserving sometimes end up with the best spouses? Why do the greedy who only think about themselves keep getting wealthier? Why do the spoiled and selfish get their college paid for? And, of course, there's the flip side. Why does the child with integrity get bullied in school? Why are the chaste and sacrificial mothers and fathers sometimes the ones who lose in divorce court to the spouse who had an affair? We could go on and on, but we don't need to because we each have an address somewhere in the world of injustice.

The stories of Haman and Mordecai highlight both sides of injustice, where the wicked prosper and the righteous suffer. *But only for a pre-determined season, and this is important.* If you love and obey Jesus, and are suffering as a result, both stories will serve as antidotes for your anguish. Let's get into the remaining verses of chapter 6.

READ ESTHER 6:11-14.

Contrast Mordecai's fortunes in Esther 4:1 with 6:11. How did his situation not just dramatically improve but reverse course?

Contrast Mordecai's actions in Esther 4:1 with Haman's in 6:12. What do you find significant?

After Haman paraded Mordecai through the city square, where did he go? How does this compare to where he went in 5:10-11?

Once Zeresh and Haman's advisors realized Haman's fortunes were dramatically changing in light of Mordecai's Jewishness—they must have had knowledge of God's remarkable preservation of the Jewish people—they start to abandon Haman. He was surrounded by fair-weather friends. They were only there for him while he was successful.

Personal Reflection: If you've surrounded yourself with people who are only there for you when you have something to offer them, what keeps you there? Conversely, if you're the type of person who only sticks by your friends or loved-ones when they have something to give you, this is the time to confess this to the Lord and commit to those God has called you to.

The beginning of Haman's demise is swift and decisive. But only if you're reading the story. If you were Mordecai, Esther, or the Jews living the story, there was nothing quick or obvious about Haman's end. I imagine they must have, at some point, questioned God's sovereignty, or wondered why responsible Mordecai was passed over for terrible Haman. Perhaps Esther agonized over how she ended up in a harem, or whether or not God would show up in this wildly pagan empire where women were used and discarded and the drunk and dastardly ended up with all the power.

Many years before Esther, a Levite named Asaph crafted some very specific questions into a psalm for the Lord that relates well to Esther 6.

READ PSALM 73.

The psalmist Asaph focuses on the wicked in verses 3-12. In verses 13-16 he turns his sights on himself and details his struggles as a righteous person. Then, in verses 17-28, he turns his gaze toward God, gaining God's perspective on both the wicked and the righteous.

In a sentence, what is Asaph's biggest complaint about the wicked (vv. 3-12)?

What is his biggest complaint about his life as a righteous person (vv. 13-16)?

What is the ultimate end of the ungodly (in New Testament terms, those who have rejected Christ, vv. 18-20,27)?

What is the ultimate end of the godly (in New Testament terms, those who are in Christ, vv. 23-28)?

Asaph expresses the grief and perplexity we all feel when the undeserving prosper. He invites us on a journey that starts in anger and confusion and ends in consolation and deeper understanding. It's not until He goes into the house of the Lord that He gains the bigger picture, discovering, "Present realities are not ultimate realities."[5] One of the most encouraging features of Psalm 73 is that even though Asaph's circumstances didn't change, he changed.

Personal Reflection:

Describe what caused the change in Asaph's heart and perspective (v. 17).

How can turning your attention to the Lord in prayer and worship, and gathering with His people change your perspective of the injustice you may be experiencing?

PSALM 37:39-40 SAYS,

The salvation of the righteous is from the Lord, their refuge in a time of distress. The Lord helps and delivers them; he will deliver them from the wicked and will save them because they take refuge in him.

LOOK BACK AT ESTHER 6:13.

When Zeresh learned that Mordecai was Jewish and that Haman was beginning to fall before him she determined that her husband's downfall was "certain." This is an important theological concept for us to understand. Even a Gentile such as Zeresh recognized that Mordecai had with him the God of the Jews.[6] Much earlier in Israel's history, the Gentile Rahab recognized the power and majesty of Israel's God (Josh. 2:8-11). And in Daniel 2:46-47, King Nebuchadnezzar bowed before Daniel, proclaiming that Daniel's God was Lord of kings and God of gods. Zeresh is another outsider in a long list who could spot the power of Israel's God at work in another's life.

As we consider Haman's downfall and Mordecai's rise to a place of honor, we must look first and foremost to God and His hand in the story. As Christ followers, we don't subscribe to a vague idea that eventually good things happen to good people and bad things happen to bad people because somehow it all shakes out in the end. In other words, Mordecai wasn't paraded around on horseback and draped in the king's robes because he was a good guy who finally got his due; rather, his fortunes changed because God chose to execute deliverance and justice based on His covenant promise to Israel. Though God blesses obedience, His mercy hangs on His righteous acts toward us, not on our moral choices.

Mordecai was clothed in the king's royal robes, an act that identified him with the king's power and position. We, too, have been given a royal inheritance, though ours is eternal.

GOSPEL MOMENT

READ 1 PETER 1:3-10.

What promises are guaranteed to you because of Christ?

Personal Reflection: What encouragement do you find to persevere through trials, knowing that your future is secure and certain?

As New Testament believers, our lives are bound up in the life of Christ. While unbelievers may prosper through ill-gotten means, and we may suffer for doing what is right, our present and future are secure. The Lord will never leave or forsake us. The wicked will eventually get their due. And those who are in Christ will be rewarded and, as Peter says, guarded.

This week we considered the rise of God's people and the demise of His enemies. You will remember from earlier in our study that Mordecai descended from King Saul of Israel and Haman from King Agag of the Amalekites (see pp. 43,59). The Amalekites were the chief enemy of the Israelites, a people group that God promised would eventually be destroyed (Num. 24:20). They were allowed to wield pain and havoc for generations, but only until the Lord determined their time was up.

We are not always good at looking to God's present promises, or the ones that will be fulfilled in the future. We need to be better at this! We do well to interpret our current struggles in light of what is currently true *and* ultimately coming in full. The truth is, you are shielded in God's power until Christ's coming. The King's love and familial loyalty has been bestowed upon you. Your inheritance can never fade. And your future is secure because of the victory Jesus has already won. As Haman's downfall was certain, your position in Christ is certain. Not because of what you've done, but because of what Jesus has accomplished for you.

Personal Reflection: What has ministered to you the most about this week that's taken place in between two banquets?

Lemon Cream Sauce Pasta with Grilled Chicken

My friends Scott and Kathy brought this dish to my house when I was in the middle of seminary finals. It is so delicious, I unashamedly ate leftovers for three days. It's a refresh on chicken and pasta, which most of us can use. So it only seemed right to ask Scott if he would share his secret lemon cream sauce recipe with my Esther friends. Thankfully, he said yes. Here's to having leftovers.

INGREDIENTS

- 4 chicken breasts, grilled
- 16 oz. pasta (Rotini or whatever you prefer)
- 1 stick of butter
- Juice from 3 lemons (more or less to taste)

- 4 egg yolks
- 1/4 tsp salt
- 4 cups heavy cream

DIRECTIONS

Grill chicken breasts to your liking. Boil pasta per directions.

FOR CREAM SAUCE: Melt butter in medium/large saucepan. Gradually whisk in heavy cream. Slowly bring to a boil (watch it closely, it can boil over quickly). Bring just to a boil and then remove from heat. Stir a small amount of the cream mixture into the egg yolks (to temper them and keep the eggs from scrambling). Then slowly stir the tempered eggs back into the cream mixture in the saucepan. Add salt and lemon juice to taste. Whisk together well and serve over pasta.

Watch the Session Five Video

Use the space below to follow along with the outline points from Kelly's teaching. A leader guide is available for free download at **lifeway.com/estherstudy**.

1. If you are looking to _____, _____, and _____ to satisfy, then you will be perpetually disappointed.

2. Don't mistake being passed over _____ for being passed over _____.

3. Sometimes God needs to get you _____ _____ for Him to do His work in your life.

To access the video sessions, use the instructions in the back of your Bible study book.

A Great Reversal

Forward *in the* Right Direction

ESTHER 7:1-10

We welcome Esther back to our study this week. I hope you have missed her as much as I have. We last saw the queen in verse 5:8, where she requested a follow-up banquet with King Ahasuerus and Haman. A lot has happened since that moment, but nothing that directly involved Esther or Mordecai's presence or immediate activity. The following quote describes this perfectly.

> *By separating the pivot point of the peripety [unexpected reversal] in Esther from the point of highest dramatic tension,* the characters of the story are not spotlighted as the cause of the reversal. *This reinforces the message that no one in the story, not even the most powerful person in the empire, is in control of what is about to happen. An unseen power is controlling the reversal of destiny.*[1] *(Emphasis mine.)*

God is always working, even when we're not. He is active even when we should be but aren't, when we want to be but can't, when we're far away, ill, or asleep.

READ ESTHER 7:1-5.

The king asked Esther to make her request known. Was this the *first*, *second*, *third*, or *fourth* time he had asked her to do this? (Circle the correct answer.)

Esther asked the king for two things. FILL IN THE BLANKS BELOW. She asked the king to:

Spare _____

Spare _____

TRUE OR FALSE? Esther specifically revealed her ethnicity and the ethnicity of her people to the king in verse 4.

Personal Take: What tactful aspects of Esther's approach stand out to you? Note the way she approaches the king and her choice of words.

Esther could have sought to save her life only, but instead she sought to spare all of her people. One of the hallmarks of our Western culture is taking care of ourselves first. *Have you loved yourself today? What would make you happy? Be true to yourself above all else.* Of course we are to love and care for ourselves—we are beloved by Christ and made in God's image. Self-care is not selfish, it's responsible. At the same time, we are called to put the interests of others above our own (Phil. 2:3-4). We're to be the kind of friends and spouses who take the posture of someone willing to wash another's feet (Matt. 13:1-16). We're to actively look for ways we can serve (Mark 10:45).

Personal Reflection: Who in your life has God put on your heart to sacrifice for and pour into? What does this practically look like?

King Ahasuerus was unclear about *who* constituted the group of people in peril. He was uncertain about Queen Esther's ethnicity. And he couldn't imagine who could have devised such a dreadful plan under his own nose. He was surprised by the whole affair! But how could the king be in the dark when he was the one who signed the decree to destroy the Jews?

LOOK BACK AT ESTHER 3:8-11. What in these verses reveals why the king was stunned by Esther's revelation in chapter 7?

There's a fine line between micromanaging those you oversee and giving your authority away. We've already seen how irresponsible the king has been with his authority. Not only did he not shepherd the people under him, he was easily manipulated by those desperate for his power and position.

Personal Reflection: Think for a moment about the impact of good leadership. Think of a good leader in your life who helped guide you, while also giving you freedom.

What traits did they model?

How did you benefit?

If we've learned nothing else about this Persian king, we know he is easily manipulated and gives his power away when he perceives his ego or wealth will benefit. When Haman falsely accused an unspecified people of being a threat to the king and offered to pay for their destruction, it took no time for Ahasuerus to lend his signet ring to Haman so he could send out the deadly edict. This will prove to be a tricky position for the king, or as my grandfather was fond of saying, "a sticky wicket." (If you've never heard this phrase because you're not yet eighty-three, the next section of reading will make its meaning plain).

READ ESTHER 7:6-10.

Where did the king go when he discovered that Haman was the one who had threatened Esther's life and the lives of an entire people group?

Why do you think he stepped out for a time?

The king was stuck! He was in a quandary of his own making. How could he punish Haman for a plot he approved? If he did, he would be admitting guilt.[2] Moreover, the king's decree was irrevocable. How could he rescind that which could not be taken back?[3]

He had inadvertently approved a plan that would destroy his wife. This, my friends, is a sticky wicket. One even the most powerful man in the empire could not extricate himself from.

> In your own words, describe what happened between Haman and Esther while the king stepped out into the palace garden.

> Look closely at verse 8. Haman is hung on the gallows because:

| He tried to kill Esther | He tried to kill the Jews | He tried to violate Esther | He tried to kill Mordecai |

We know from Persian protocol that no one but the king was to be left alone with a woman from the harem.[4] Haman should have left Esther's presence when the king left the room. But Haman was desperate. He needed Esther to persuade the king to show him mercy. In his desperation, he fell on the couch where Esther was sitting, and when the king reentered the room it appeared Haman was trying to rape or abuse her.

Many commentators do not believe this is what Haman was doing, nor do they believe the king actually thought this was what Haman was doing. Regardless of intent, the appearance of evil gave the king the out he needed. Haman received the punishment he deserved but for the wrong crime.[5] This was the perfect scenario for the king—he rid himself of Haman on account of sexual assault and saved face in doing so, since he too was party to the tragic edict that set itself against his own wife and her people. "Once again, ignorance, misapprehension, and bungling move events forward in the right direction."[6]

Personal Reflection: Think about a time when you saw God "move events forward in the right direction" through the most unlikely, even disastrous, of circumstances. What did you learn about God's nature through that experience? Detail who you found Him to be.

As a Bible teacher, specifically one who delights in helping make Scripture practical, Esther is a challenging book to teach. Not only is there no mention of God, His people worshiping in the temple, or the Scripture (the Torah) guiding their steps, but scenes like this one are characterized by rage, scandal, and murder. Try making a sentimental share square out of this passage—*You can trust God's sovereignty in your banquet disasters*. But, is this actually the perfect sentiment to point to?

Most of the story details the Lord's activity working through the depravity of humanity—who can't relate to that? While this is somewhat frustrating from a moral-of-the-story standpoint, it's refreshing from a theological one: God is pleased to reach into the darkest corners of our world to accomplish His purposes on behalf of His people. He brings resolution, even if through an odd series of anger, fumbling, bumbling, and happenstance.

Personal Reflection: How are you encouraged or challenged by God's hand at work even in the dark and messy scene of Esther 7?

Haman was hanged on the very gallows he built for Mordecai. His rise upward swiftly turned to a harrowing fall downward. God's sovereign hand was moving everything "forward in the right direction," after all.

Today is a day to respond to God's unfathomable sovereignty. He is not only the God of the Jews, or God over the Persian empire; He is Lord over the cosmos. Jesus Christ is holding all things together. When life is hard and we're tempted to go low into despair, as my friend Selma Wilson says, "this is when we go high." Yes, we carry heavy burdens, anxieties swirl about our minds, and sometimes the circumstances we find ourselves in are nothing but chaotic. This is where we look up. This is where we go to the One who has the whole world in His hands.

GOSPEL MOMENT

READ COLOSSIANS 1:15-20.

Personal Response: Take time with these verses and respond to Jesus's sovereignty over your life and over all creation.

Finishing *a* Job Left Undone

ESTHER 7:5-10

The story of Esther is a distinct combination of human courage and divine activity. While Esther and Mordecai stepped up when they needed to and sacrificially placed their lives on the line, it's plainly obvious that God was the one orchestrating the events at hand.

Personal Reflection: How does this reality encourage you to work hard and obey, while trusting that God will accomplish His will in your life? Do you tend to lean more one way than the other?

READ ESTHER 7:5-10. We're revisiting these verses from yesterday.

What verb is used to describe what Haman was doing on the couch that Esther was sitting on?

Falling   Sitting   Laying   Standing

LOOK BACK AT ESTHER 6:13. What similar description did Zeresh use to predict Haman's demise?

What did Mordecai refuse to do for Haman in 3:2? And how does this add irony to the scene in 7:8?

After Haman paraded Mordecai through the city square, Zeresh could see that Haman's status was crumbling, and his ultimate downfall was certain. Now, Haman is falling before Esther on the couch, pleading for his life. The same Hebrew word for *fall* is used in each passage. That the word is used in both places highlights that the fall previously hinted at is now happening on a grand scale.[7] It's also ironic that Haman couldn't persuade Mordecai the Jew to fall before him, yet now Haman is falling before Esther, a Jew.

This full-circle moment makes for great storytelling, but more importantly, it's a reminder that our God is faithful to His promises to defend the righteous and deal justly with the wicked. These 180-degree reversals are meant to show God's ultimate justice on behalf of His people.[8] They remind us that God's hand is on the story from beginning to end. And His hand is on your life, too.

LOOK BACK AT ESTHER 7:8-10.

Who told the king about the gallows Haman had built?

What did the king command in response to this information?

Personal Take: What three characteristics would you use to describe the king in this scene?

Yet again, the king is in the dark, the servants know more about what is going on in palace life than he does, and his response is hasty and reactionary. This is not the first time his anger has dictated his decisions, nor the first time we've seen him need time to cool down. In chapter 1, he raged when Vashti refused to exploit herself before him and his nobles. He only settled down after he'd deposed her and sent out a rash decree for the men to take charge of their wives at home. Incidentally, it will soon be Esther, a woman, from whom the king will be taking orders.

READ PROVERBS 26:27,

The one who digs a pit will fall into it, and whoever rolls a stone—it will come back on him.

How does Esther 7:10 display the truth of Proverbs 26:27?

READ 2 PETER 2:9,

Then the Lord knows how to rescue the godly from trials and to keep the unrighteous under punishment for the day of judgment.

What does the Lord do for the godly and the ungodly?

Take a moment to sit with the divine reversal of Esther 7:10. While Jesus makes clear we're to love and pray for our enemies, the New Testament writers also encourage the righteous sufferer to take heart that God deals with those who come against us unjustly.

Personal Reflection: You may be having a hard time with someone who's causing you pain. You may also feel that you're never going to get free of the trial you're in. How do 2 Peter 2:9 and Esther 7:10 encourage you?

Some commentators feel that Esther's lack of compassion toward Haman was a moral failure on her part. They think she should have had mercy on Haman, like David had on King Saul. I disagree with this perspective for a few reasons, but one in particular. We've already learned about the age-old rivalry between Israel represented by Mordecai, and the Amalekites represented by Haman. But I want to look at a monumental moment in Israel's history that may very well link straight to Esther 7:10.

TURN BACK TO 1 SAMUEL AND READ CHAPTER 15. Settle in. It's an important story to know.

What did Saul leave undone?

God values _____ over sacrifice (v. 22, FILL IN THE BLANK).

What happened to Saul as a result of his disobedience to the Lord?

The prophet Samuel killed Agag, but the Amalekites survived to fight against Israel for generations. Their specialty? Attacking the weak, vulnerable, women, and children.[9] "By designing the death of Haman the Agagite, Queen Esther has succeeded where her ancestor King Saul had failed, whether or not she was aware of it."[10] And you know what? Haman is the last reference to Amalek in the Old Testament.[11] Esther finished what Saul had left undone.

As Christ followers we are called to go the extra mile, forgive, and pray for our enemies (Matt 5:38-48). We are also called to put to death, or put an end to, sinful and harmful behaviors and activities. Perhaps there is a generational sin in your family that you know you can no longer tolerate. Maybe someone's behavior is disrupting your home or workplace and you need to lovingly address it. Maybe you've turned a blind eye to an injustice that you can no longer ignore. Whether or not Esther knew she was participating in God's promise to blot out the Amalekites, the message is powerful: She took care of what her ancestors had not.

GOSPEL MOMENT

SPEND TIME REFLECTING ON EPHESIANS 6:10-18.

We don't wage war with seventy-five-foot gallows, but we do fight against the devil's schemes with "weapons" of a different kind. Contrast the ways that Paul encourages us to fight against evil versus in Esther's day.

Personal Reflection: What in your history, or family's history, has been left undone that the Holy Spirit is bringing to mind? What pieces of spiritual armor do you need to put on?

Esther finished a job that should have been completed generations before her. We, too, are compelled to deal with the sin in our lives that may have lingered far too long. We are able to do this because of Jesus's final work on the cross—He finished the job no one else could. Thankfully, putting to death the sin in our midst doesn't require physical weapons, rather obedience to Christ and the power of the Holy Spirit. As God's children, it is our privilege to meekly and courageously put an end to what hinders our (and our loved ones') walk with Christ. What a vivid picture of this Esther leaves us with today.

An Irrevocable Decree

ESTHER 8:1-9

A major stake was driven into the ground yesterday. Haman's death spelled the end of the Amalekites, the Jews' chief enemies in the Persian empire. Unfortunately, a problem still existed. While Haman was dead, his evil and hostility had outlived him.

READ ESTHER 8:1-2.

What did Ahasuerus give Esther the same day that Haman was hanged?

Who entered the king's presence and why?

What did the king give Mordecai?

With a little imagination, this is quite a sentimental moment. Years prior it was Mordecai who had compassion on his orphaned cousin. He could have passed Esther off to another family member—surely someone else was better suited to care for her. After all, didn't he have enough to manage in a foreign world without the burden of raising a child?

We can reasonably assume the Jews in Persia had access to, or at least knowledge of, God's law. While not every aspect of the law could be practiced in a foreign land (worship in the temple and sacrifices, for instance), certain elements could be carried out anywhere.

READ DEUTERONOMY 24:17-22.

How did Mordecai personalize God's command in verses 17-18?

What of God's delivering acts did He want His people to remember every time they looked after the vulnerable?

Evidently, Mordecai took God's commands about caring for orphans seriously. He took Esther as his own, having no idea how it would turn out. All these years later, Esther was now in a position to bless Mordecai in return. His relationship to her was what granted him a place in the palace and the king's signet ring.

If only the story ended here. The evil Haman hung on his own gallows, the orphaned, ethnic outcast turned queen of Persia holding keys to Haman's estate, and Mordecai wearing the king's signet ring. And they all lived happily . . . wait, the story isn't over yet.

Though the king gave Esther and Mordecai lavish and unexpected gifts, these aren't what Esther requested in verse 7:3. What still remained *undone*?

KEEP READING ESTHER 8:3-9.

In verses 3 and 5, Esther begs the king to *revoke* the evil plot of Haman the Agagite (CSB). Some versions say "reverse," "overrule," or "put an end to."

But what is stated in 8:8 (and hinted at in 1:19) about decrees recorded in the laws of Persia and Media?

Verses 5-6 make clear that no matter what happened with the fate of the Jews, Esther was safe. The king was acting favorably toward her and had given her Haman's estate. But this was not enough for Esther. She was not content to sit back simply because her life was no longer in danger while her people were still in jeopardy.

Personal Reflection: When all is going well for us it's easy to forget the suffering of others and how significant our time and attention can be to those who are hurting. How does Esther's selflessness challenge or inspire you?

The reality for Esther, Mordecai, and the Jews was that, even though Haman was dead, his genocidal edict was alive and well and could not be rescinded. The king could give Esther up to half his kingdom, but he couldn't undo his own decree! He was caught in the tendrils of his own making. *No one is truly free in the empire.*

Look back at verses 8-9. Since the king can't revoke his decree against the Jews, what does he give Esther and Mordecai permission to do instead?

While the king couldn't rescind Haman's decree, he did allow Esther and Mordecai to send out a decree of their own, one that would positively affect the Jews. We often can't undo the evil in our world, but we can counteract it with good (Rom. 12:21). I have the privilege of working with vulnerable children in Moldova alongside Justice & Mercy International. Many of the teenagers I've spent time with there have grown up in abusive homes, some were abandoned at young ages. Our Moldovan staff can't undo the atrocities that have been done to these precious children, but they can pour love into each child who walks through their doors. Goodness can't always undo evil, but it can overcome it.

Personal Response: Think of a specific situation you wish you could undo for someone but know you can't. How can you actively bring goodness and love to the situation?

That the king cannot undo his deadly decree but will allow Mordecai and Esther to write a life-saving decree of their own foreshadows a future momentous event. At just the right time, after the irrevocable consequences of sin entered the world and all manner of death and destruction followed, God issued "a counter-decree of life, the Gospel of Jesus Christ."[12] Based on God's justice, He could not simply undo the consequences of sin's entrance into our world, but He could send His beloved Son to bear our sin for us.

GOSPEL MOMENT

The Gospel of Jesus is the "counter-decree" to the ultimate consequences of sin. Reflect on each passage and write what ministers to you the most about Christ's sacrifice.

1 JOHN 4:9-12

ROMANS 5:6-8

Today's scene in Esther feels a lot like everyday life to me. Well, not the part about being a queen, or confronting a king, or living in a palace, or pleading on behalf of an entire people group. It's the part about how everything is sort-of tied up, but not fully. Yes, Ahasuerus responded favorably to Esther and, yes, he gave her Haman's estate, and, no, he wasn't angry that both Esther and Mordecai had withheld their familial relationship from him, or that they were Jews. All of this is fantastic news. But, big sigh, things are still far from resolved.

A dangerous and irrevocable decree was floating about, one the king couldn't care less about. And Esther, Mordecai, and the Jews didn't know how this whole thing was going to end. And *that* is the part that feels like everyday life—the we-have-some-good-news-but-we're-not-out-of-the-woods-yet sort of experience. When we feel this tension, we must actively choose to put our hope and trust in the Lord, the One who does know how it will all end, who is in control, and who has His hand on our lives and the lives of those we care about.

Scholars often refer to this tension as living in the "already but not yet." The kingdom of God has indeed come to earth. We have the power of the Spirit living within us. Christ has conquered sin on the cross. Still, we await the full measure of His coming kingdom. When Jesus returns all sin, sickness, and death will be put to a final end, and all heaven and earth will be renewed.

READ 1 PETER 5:6-7.

Personal Response: Peter was writing to a group of suffering believers when he penned these verses. How does verse 7 in particular encourage you to trust the Lord in the unknowns of your current circumstances?

Rest in the assurance that the one who holds the future is all-powerful, all-knowing, all-present, and good. Don't let your fears hold you back from what God is calling you to do. You have no idea what blessings lay on the other side.

A Messy Counter-Decree

ESTHER 8:9-14

Today's passage is not the most well-known and certainly not the most heartwarming in the book of Esther. While the final two chapters culminate in celebration, it will not come without a brutal fight. Esther, Mordecai, and the Jews had most certainly hoped the king would overturn Haman's edict and render it null and void. But, as we learned yesterday, this was against Persian law. We will discover today that the Jews would have to participate in their own deliverance. And while not the most cherished of Scripture passages, today will offer us a cherished principle: When God comes to our rescue, He often invites our participation.

READ ESTHER 8:9-14.

Summarize the main points of Mordecai's edict in your own words (v. 11).

On what day was this to take place, and over how many days (v. 12)?

How does Mordecai's edict (v. 12) compare with Haman's (3:13)?

Haman's and Mordecai's edicts mirror each other with opposite intentions. The parallel helps show that as quickly as someone can rise to power and impose harm, he or she can just as quickly lose power and be replaced.[13] It also emphasizes a grand reversal of fortune for the Jews and Mordecai in particular. But it won't be a neat and tidy reversal.

Personal Take: Look back at Esther 8:11-12. If you were a Jew living under Haman's edict of looming destruction, what about this text would give you hope? What about it might add stress to your life and family, or at the very least make you heavy hearted?

Personal Take: What do you find troubling, if anything, about verse 8:11?

Commentators wrestle with what to make of women and children being slaughtered. Different translations take different approaches. The NIV positions the women and children as belonging to the Jews. The Jews were "to destroy, kill and annihilate the armed men of any nationality or province who might attack them and their women and children." The CSB, on the other hand, poses that the Jews could "destroy, kill, and annihilate every ethnic and provincial army hostile to them, including women and children."

Commentators are split on how to translate the Hebrew, which is why different translations take different approaches. If we take the most troubling scenario—that the Jews can kill the women and children of the men who attack them—we need to at least keep three things in mind.

First, Mordecai's edict was not a license for indiscriminate bloodshed. The Jews could only destroy the men, and the families of the men, who came against them, and this was limited to a single day (a merciful boundary). And because every people group in the Persian empire was made aware of this provision for the Jews, they knew what they were exposing their families to if they decided to come against the Jewish people. Second, just because the edict made provision for the Jews to attack women and children (if this is the correct reading) didn't mean the Jews would necessarily carry this out. And third, for us as followers of Christ, Jesus radically redefined the Old Testament law that allowed for exact measures of retaliation (Lev. 24:19-21).

TURN TO MATTHEW 5:38-42. How did Jesus reframe the idea of paying someone back in the exact way they harmed you?

Whatever we make of Esther 8:11, and however we understand Jesus's words in Matthew 5:38-42, one thing is for certain: we are not free to violently get even for the sake of revenge. Furthermore, we need Jesus to form us into people who pray for our enemies and bless those who persecute us. John Stott says about Jesus's words here, "Nowhere is the challenge of the Sermon greater. Nowhere is the distinctness of the Christian counter-culture more obvious."[14] Loving one's enemies in the Persian empire would have stood out just the way it does today, in our twenty-first-century world!

Personal Prayer: Who are you having trouble praying for because he or she has hurt you? Before moving on in today's study, pray about this situation according to Jesus's words.

According to Esther 8:11, the king's edict gave the Jews the right to *assemble*. In Old Testament times the Jews assembled for military, political, and judicial purposes, and also for worship. This may have been the first time the Jews in Persia were allowed to gather together like this. They wouldn't win this battle scattered abroad as individuals.

Like the Jews in the Persian empire, we need the body of believers in our lives today. We need each other to win the battles we're facing. Hebrews 10:24-25 says, "Let us consider one another in order to provoke love and good works, not neglecting to *gather together*, as some are in the habit of doing, but encouraging each other, and all the more as you see the day approaching" (emphasis mine).

Personal Response: What area of your life are you trying to handle yourself instead of asking other believers for help? Who is the Holy Spirit bringing to your mind to reach out to?

The Jews assembling together shows that their participation with God is essential to their redemption. God could have revoked Haman's edict with a snap of His fingers, but He didn't choose to do so. Instead, He gave Mordecai and Esther the positional power to issue a counter-decree, one that would require the Jews to come together and fight a battle of justice.

Personal Reflection:

Describe a time when God pulled you out of a difficult or impossible situation that required virtually no effort on your part.

Describe a time when God asked you to participate in the rescue and restoration He was bringing about in your life. What is one specific area you grew in as a result?

We often want our healing to take place straightaway. And while God can accomplish anything at any moment, more times than not He empowers us to *participate* with Him in our sanctification (sanctification is growing to be more and more like Christ). This is an individual as well as a corporate journey. The sanctification journey may look many different ways. It may require getting a job in a time in life you weren't expecting to. It may mean getting into counseling in order to walk away from a destructive habit. It could be buckling down on excess spending to get out of debt. You may need to change your diet or start exercising to get healthy. Whatever God is asking you to do, it is always for His glory and your freedom.

GOSPEL MOMENT

READ 1 PETER 1:13-23.

Personal Response: What active steps of obedience is the Lord asking you to take as you set your heart fully on the grace that will be revealed when Jesus returns (1 Pet. 1:13)?

I'm so grateful for the times God has reached down to pluck me straight out of hardship. He has done it in my past, and He will do it again. But more often than not my active obedience is a necessary ingredient in my healing and deliverance. What I have learned is that when He draws me into a process of refining and sanctification, I change, I get to know Him more intimately, and I become more like Him. May we join the Lord in whatever He is doing in our hearts and lives today. And like the Jewish people, may we *assemble* with the community of believers. We're not meant to live the Christian life alone!

A Series of Reversals

ESTHER 8:15-17; 9:1

I have a dear friend in the Amazon who is teaching himself English and practices whenever he has the chance. He's also fallen in love with American football. Naturally, I talked him into becoming a Tennessee Titans fan. During a recent game when the Titans were losing (this has been happening entirely too frequently as of late), he texted me, "Let's reverse the score!" His phrasing made me ponder what exactly a reversal is. It is not a mere improvement of circumstances or even a change in score. Reversals are an about face of direction, where the outcome turns out to be the mirror opposite of what was expected.

The literary term used to describe reversals is *peripety*, which refers "to a sudden turn of events that reverses the expected outcome of a story."[15] We see layers of peripety all throughout the book of Esther. We have addressed these reversals briefly along the way, but we haven't focused on the theme as a whole. We will do that today. As we go, we must ask some questions. What is significant about reversals in Scripture? Why do they matter? And what is God telling us about Himself and His ultimate plan for the world in the telling of divine reversals?

READ ESTHER 8:15-17.

Compare the couplets below. List the reversals you see in the lives of Mordecai, the Jews, and the city of Susa (capital of Persia).

MORDECAI	JEWS	CITIZENS OF SUSA
4:1-2 with 8:15	4:3 with 8:16-17	3:15 with 8:15

Personal Reflection: Think back over the book of Esther. What is the most meaningful reversal you can think of and why? It may help you to think in pairs, such as Esther and Mordecai, Esther and Vashti, Haman and Mordecai, the Jews and the Persians, and so on.

LOOK MORE CLOSELY AT ESTHER 8:15. Who celebrates the reversal in Mordecai's life?

The Jews were not the only ones celebrating Mordecai's rise to power. All the city of Susa was rejoicing! Far from resenting the appointment of Mordecai, a foreign minority, the people were thrilled.[16]

NOW READ PROVERBS 29:2. How do these verses speak to what's happening in Persia in Esther 8:15-17?

Personal Take: What does God's authoring of the reversals in Esther tell us about the outcomes of the righteous and the unrighteous? Go beneath a surface response.

Surrounding books of the Bible shed light on the events and themes of Esther, which help us faithfully interpret the book's meaning. Much earlier in Israel's history, right before the beginning of Israel's monarchy and long before the exile, a woman named Hannah prayed a prayer of praise and thanksgiving after God opened her once barren womb and gave her a son she had longed and prayed for. Hannah's prayer highlights the motif of reversals perhaps more than any other in the Old Testament.

READ 1 SAMUEL 2:1-10.

Personal Take: What is one reversal in Hannah's prayer that could be applied to any main character in Esther? Write it below with the person's name beside it.

Look at 1 Samuel 2:8b and FILL IN THE BLANKS. The Lord has set the world on _____. The foundation (or pillars) of the world belong to _____.

Hannah's prayer reveals that God's sovereignty is at the center of these kinds of reversals.[17] When God works about-face wonders, whether in Hannah's life, Esther's, Mordecai's, Haman's, or our own, He's showing His good justice over our lives and in our world.

Personal Prayer: Where do you long to see God's justice and sovereignty in your life or in the life of another? Spend time praying over this. Use Hannah's prayer as a prayer prompt for your own.

The arrogant who exalt themselves and oppress the poor will be brought low (Haman), while the humble poor in the dust heap will be seated with nobles (Mordecai). The bows of the wicked are broken (Ahasuerus was eventually murdered by his vizier), while the feeble are clothed with strength (Esther). It is precisely God's mighty hand of bringing down the proud and exalting the lowly—in all its many forms—that directly coincides with the just foundation upon which He has set our world.

Just this morning I thanked God for a reversal He brought about in my life nearly twenty years ago. I was financially scraping by, I was barely making it as a singer/songwriter, and the friends I had surrounded myself with weren't walking in God-honoring ways. I was lonely, anxious, and fighting depression. The rescue God brought about in my life isn't a short story, but it can be summed up in Hannah's song—He raised me from the trash heap (1 Sam. 2:8). It is true that these changes did not happen overnight. And it is also true that some of my longings have yet to be met. But I am often brought to tears over the ways God picked me up and brought about a series of tangible reversals that astound me even today.

READ ESTHER 9:1. This is the farthest-reaching reversal in the book. Describe it in your own words.

In many ways, the book of Esther leads up to this moment. It's the grandest and most sweeping reversal of them all. As we consider God's rescue of His people, we can see in hindsight that any physical and spiritual reversals at work in Esther are mere shadows of the ultimate reversal still to come in Christ. We will get to that next week. In the meantime, be encouraged that part of Jesus's very ministry to you is a ministry of reversals—darkness to light, mourning to celebration, death to life.

GOSPEL MOMENT

READ LUKE 4:16-21.

What reversals did Jesus highlight from Isaiah 61 in verses 18-19?

Jesus declared that the prophecy from Isaiah has now been (circle below):

Changed   Renewed   Fulfilled   Rescinded

Personal Reflection: How has today's focus on God's ability to bring about redemptive reversals encouraged you? Be specific.

It turns out that many of the people to whom Jesus read the scroll in the synagogue that day would reject Him. They didn't regard Him as the Messiah who would bring about the release of captives, restore sight to the blind, or set free the oppressed. But we believe He is the Messiah, one who has brought about a kingdom in which the arrogant will ultimately be brought low, and the poor in spirit who find their riches in Christ will be raised up. *This* is the foundation upon which He has set the world. The oppressive Hamans and the reckless Ahasueruses will falter and ultimately fade away. But those in Christ will prevail.

Fresh Summer Salad
with Roasted Chicken

I made this for the girls who helped test-run the Esther manuscript. It was on a day when I felt a little hurried and needed something easy to throw together quickly. I wasn't expecting their overwhelming enthusiasm for . . . a salad. But enthused they were. It made me think that maybe we're skimping on a few ingredients that can take a salad over the top. So here goes!

INGREDIENTS FOR SALAD

- Large bag or a couple heads of your favorite lettuce (I like the baby kale and spinach mix, gem lettuce, or torn romaine)

- 1 rotisserie chicken, carved into bite-sized pieces

- 1 large orange or red bell pepper, diced or sliced long-ways

- 1 English cucumber, chopped

- Cherry tomatoes, cut in half

- 1-2 avocados, sliced into half-moon pieces

- Feta cheese, 8 oz.

INGREDIENTS FOR DRESSING

- ¾ cup olive oil

- ¼ cup red wine vinegar

- 1 tsp minced garlic

- 1 tsp dried oregano

- 1 tsp dried basil

- ½ tsp onion powder

- ½ tsp crushed red pepper

- ¾ tsp salt

- ½ tsp pepper

- 2 tsp juice from lemon

DIRECTIONS

Fill your salad bowl with lettuce greens. On top, place chicken, bell pepper, cucumber, tomatoes, avocado, and feta in their own piles. This gives a fresh and colorful look. Salt and pepper the chicken and vegetables. Cover and set aside if guests are arriving within 30 minutes (refrigerate if longer, but leave tomatoes off since they don't like to be refrigerated). When ready to eat, toss the salad thoroughly in the dressing and serve.

Watch the Session Six Video

Use the space below to follow along with the outline points from Kelly's teaching. A leader guide is available for free download at **lifeway.com/estherstudy**.

1. The effects of our _____ can outlive us, but so

can the effects of our _____.

2. When all is well _____, we need to be

concerned about what is not well _____.

3. No matter the weight of your sin it is not more powerful than

God's counter-decree of the _____.

To access the video sessions, use the instructions in the back of your Bible study book.

A
Great
Celebration

SESSION SEVEN

Things Turned

About

ESTHER 9:1-10

By now we're familiar with the overlap in timelines between the books of Nehemiah, Ezra, and Esther. When I wrote my third Bible study on the book of Nehemiah, I was perplexed about how to treat the ending. We are a people, at least in my experience, who want our literature and movies to end happily, or at the very least hopefully. But Nehemiah ends with one of Israel's chief enemies setting up office space in the temple, the resettled Jews desecrating the Sabbath, and the prophet so angry over the people's sin that he starts ripping people's beards out. The book of Ezra isn't much different, as the curtain closes on a complicated series of severed marriages—and during the rainy season, to make matters more depressing.

Esther covers the same era as Ezra and Nehemiah, and like its counterparts, it also ends in an odd place by our modern standards. I could offer you at least two or three "better" places at which to tie up Esther than with chapters 9 and 10. But truth be told, the aim of Old Testament books isn't a tidy ending. They aren't written for the sole purpose of depicting moral examples of how we're to live, though there are countless people from whom we can learn deeply. Rather, they show us how everyday human beings sometimes get it right but oftentimes don't, and how God is sovereign and faithful all along the way.

With Esther in particular, it's important for us to remember that one of the author's main objectives was to show *why* the Jews celebrate Purim, or better yet *how* the holiday came to be. This is considered the "etiology" of Esther. (An *etiology* is "a story that explains the origin of an event."[1]) This may not be a burning question for us today, but it was for the original readers and the Jews who have celebrated Purim ever since.

Now that we've aligned our expectations with one of the story's major aims, let's get to the most "exciting" part of Esther—*The End*.

Last week, we focused on the theme of reversals. Esther 9:1 describes the farthest-reaching reversal of all. "On the day when the Jews' enemies had hoped to overpower them, just the opposite happened. The Jews overpowered those who hated them" (9:1b). One way to translate a portion of this verse is, "*Things would be turned about*, in that the Jews gained control over their adversaries"[2] (emphasis mine). Things would be turned about! I love that imagery.

The Jews had, at one point, anticipated that on the thirteenth day of Adar their enemies would overpower them (Esth. 3:13). Instead, they are the ones who do the overpowering. Perhaps by giving away the ending before recounting the details of battle the author is reminding us that with God ultimate victory is a foregone conclusion.

> Personal Reflection: Briefly write about a time when you didn't have what it took to overcome, and yet by God's grace, you overcame who or what was opposing you (even if it was a long process). What did you learn about God's faithfulness that encourages you today?

Every nationality in Persia was _____ the Jews (v. 2).

stronger than   wealthier than   afraid of   suspect of

Throughout Israel's history God often caused fear to fall upon her enemies by way of His supernatural activity in their midst (Josh. 2:9-11). But in Esther, we see God working providentially through ordinary events. It's one of Esther's hallmarks. The Red Sea hadn't split in two, but Mordecai's rise to power must have split a few political agendas in half. An exiled Jew was now second in command over the entire Persian Empire. Furthermore, Mordecai's growing fame and power is described in a similar way to another prominent leader in Israel's history. Esther 9:4 shares much in common with Exodus 11:3.[3]

READ EXODUS 11:3,

The Lord gave the people favor with the Egyptians. In addition, Moses himself was very highly regarded in the land of Egypt by Pharaoh's officials and the people.

Circle above: In what place did Moses become great?

Who gave favor to Israel as Moses led them out of Egypt?

That Mordecai's growing stature in Persia is likely linked to Moses's ascent in Egypt is significant. It reveals that, even in faraway places like Persia, God raises up men and women to guide and protect His people. What He did through Moses by delivering the Israelites He would do again through Mordecai and Esther. And He's been raising up people ever since, in every generation, in every part of our world!

Personal Response: Mordecai rose from lowly exile to second in command. Who have you seen God raise up to make a major difference in your own day? Describe the way their life has encouraged you.

God plucked Moses out of a papyrus basket and turned him into a deliverer. He transformed Mordecai from being an outsider in Persia to an insider in the palace. He saw Esther, an orphan in a harem, and gave her the queen's throne. So, too, God wants to use you for His good purposes. He sees you in your unique circumstances. He hasn't forgotten about you.

READ 1 CORINTHIANS 1:26-31. God often uses the lowly, those who know their frailty and limitations. Why is this so (vv. 29,31)?

It has been said that pride makes us either smug or small. Either we become arrogant and think too highly of ourselves or we question our worth, which is a subtler form of pride.

In both Esther and 1 Corinthians (and really throughout all of Scripture), we're shown that God delights to use the weak, the outsider, those who know they need Him. And when He does call us and empower us, we know it is Him, and we give Him the glory.

LOOK BACK AT ESTHER 9:5-9.

On the 13th of Adar the Jews killed those who _____ them.

    hated   feared   taunted   opposed

How many people died in the fortress of Susa that day? _____

Whose ten sons were killed? _____

We can talk about Mordecai's unexpected rise to power, Queen Esther's rags-to-riches saga, and the Jews' liberation, but sadly we cannot do so without talking about bloodshed. Yes, the Jews would have victory but as one Jewish scholar commented, "The resolution of this conflict is about to be paid for in blood."[4] (Do you hear the foreshadowing of another conflict whose resolution was also paid for in blood, the blood shed on a cross? We'll get to that later this week.)

It's reasonable to feel tension when reading Scripture. One of the things I love about the Bible is that it invites us to grapple with its stories. The Old Testament in particular is often descriptive not prescriptive. It describes what happened, which is very different than prescribing what everyone should do in all places for all times. As sad as this day in Susa was, we must remember two things: 1. The Jewish people fought as a result of Haman's decree. They weren't the perpetrators. 2. Only those foolish and hateful enough to come against the Jews were subject to attack. Mordecai's decree was not a license for indiscriminate killing.

Personal Take: Why do you think it was important that the Jews made sure Haman's ten sons did not survive? (Look back at page 59 for the link between Haman/the Amalekites, and King Saul/ the Israelites).

Compare Esther 9:10 with 8:11. What were the Jews allowed to do that they did not do?

Personal Take: Why do you think the Jews chose not to touch the plunder of their enemies, especially since it was allowed?

Tomorrow, we'll examine this event further as we read on, but for now I want to end where we began. Things would be "turned about" for the Jews. God chose the Jewish people as His own, made a covenant with them, and promised their survival—ensuring Haman's decree to annihilate them would ultimately fail. But I imagine this wasn't as obvious to Esther, Mordecai, or the rest of the Jews while they prepared for the 13th day of Adar as it is to us now with hindsight and the full story of Scripture. As my friend Molly said, "It's much easier to put the puzzle pieces together when God gives you the box with the picture on it." They didn't have that box.

Personal Response: Consider one promise in Scripture that you believe but don't always live as though it is reality. What step can you take today to live as though His promise is true?

The Jews in Persia had gone about their lives many miles and years removed from temple worship and religious sacrifices. Their spiritual home was an insurmountable journey away. It's reasonable to assume that while they had hoped God would deliver them, their faith may have wavered. Perhaps the author is reminding us that even when we forget God's promises, doubt them, or are living far from our spiritual homes, He remains faithful to His promises. And one day He will return, and all sickness, evil, war, and death—yes, all things contrary to His will—will be "turned about" (Rev. 21:4). What a day of rejoicing that will be.

GOSPEL MOMENT

READ ROMANS 8:17-18.

What does this passage remind you about God? How does it encourage you in whatever trial you're walking through?

Holy War

ESTHER 9:11-19

One of the challenges of studying the Old Testament is uncovering cultures and customs so different from our own. This is certainly the case as we look this week not only at war, but holy war. Doing some contextual work will help us better understand the ancient mindset and therefore receive a fresh dose of wisdom for what to do, and not do, when we're given power over those who have hurt us.

Let's begin with a word about holy war. In the Old Testament, holy war had to do with Israel fighting battles that preserved them as a nation and protected their expressions of worshiping God through sacrifices, festivals, and gatherings in the tabernacle and temple. On many occasions, God forbade war and promoted peaceful solutions. However, in some instances He commanded Israel to fully wipe out entire people groups, including their family members, livestock, and structures, dedicating what they conquered fully to the Lord (Ex 23:23-25; Josh. 6:20-21; 1 Sam. 15:2-3).[5] This does not sit comfortably with our modern sensibilities.

For one thing, Jesus Christ put an end to holy war once and for all. He was the only one just and worthy enough to wage a perfect and victorious war on sin by offering Himself on the cross as our atonement. As a result, we are no longer to persecute those who hurt us; rather, we are to pray for and bless our enemies since we now live in the power of the Holy Spirit. "True holy war in human history has ceased because Jesus has fought its last episode on the cross."[6]

> **Personal Prayer:** I know you haven't even begun our Scripture reading yet, but take a moment to thank God for His immeasurable gift of salvation, and ask Him to prepare your heart for today.

Back in Esther's day, approximately five hundred years before Jesus's incarnation, the Jews operated under a different covenant. Many of the same moral values we treasure today, such as working for peace, showing compassion to the outsider and foreigner, blessing surrounding cultures, and demonstrating generosity, were ingrained in Israel's culture by God Himself. But how Israel worked out these values was often necessarily different than how we work them out today.

In the case of the Diaspora Jews in the Persian Empire, they were the underdogs, exiles, and without power over their own land. For them, Haman represented the Amalekites, and the Amalekites represented the classic enemy of Israel. Haman's edict left unchecked would have spelled the end of God's people, but perhaps more significantly the end of God's covenant—something God was never going to let happen. With that background in mind, let's get reading!

READ ESTHER 9:11-15.

It seems that King Ahasuerus was more impressed with how many people had died in Susa and the rest of the empire than he was with the Jews gaining freedom.[7] As if people dying in battle was a pastime for him. When people in power lose sight of the people under their care, God's original intent for pure and just leadership erodes, and everyday citizens suffer.

REVISIT VERSES 13-15. What two requests did Queen Esther ask of King Ahasuerus?

REQUEST 1	REQUEST 2

How many additional people died in Susa on the 14th day of Adar?

Personal Take: What surprises you, if anything, about Esther's requests of the king?

Esther's second request is that Haman's already impaled sons be hung on gallows for everyone to see. This was a customary practice in ancient warfare. It served as public disgrace for the dead and a vivid warning for what might happen to anyone else who was planning an attack against the Jews.

Personal Take: We're not given a motive behind Esther's first request for another day of warfare. What do you make of it from a moral standpoint? Do you think Esther was or was not justified?

We are not privy to what Esther knew about lingering antisemitism in Persia or possible looming attacks from Haman's sympathizers. An extra day to finish the job could have been wisdom, as many commentators believe.[8] But it's also not out of the realm of possibility that power had gone to her head and this was nothing but revenge.[9] While I think Esther was acting prudently, the author doesn't reveal her motives. So the question I want you to sit with today is: How are you handling your influence, power, wealth, and/or resources?

READ LUKE 22:24-30. In your own words, what does Jesus require of us as we lead others?

Personal Reflection: What is one way you can stand guard against overstepping the authority God has given you?

TURN BACK TO ESTHER AND CONTINUE READING VERSES 16-19.

How many people died in the empire of Persia outside the capital of Susa? _____

The Jews outside Susa fought on the 13th day of Adar and rested and celebrated on the _____ day of Adar. And the Jews inside the city walls fought on the 13th and 14th day of Adar and rested and celebrated on the _____ day of Adar.

Those living outside Susa celebrated on the 14th day of Adar and those inside on the 15th. Each celebration occurred on the day after victory. The details of who fought when, celebrated where, and on what days may seem trivial to us, but it was important to the author to explain why Purim was celebrated on two days. It can be likened to why kindergartners learn about the Mayflower and the Pilgrims every time Thanksgiving rolls around—we need to know why we set aside an entire day to give thanks and eat turkey!

What important detail is given in verse 16 that was also noted in verses 10 and 15?

Mordecai's decree allowed the Jews to plunder their enemies but they never did so. One of the rules of ancient holy war is that plunder was not to be taken.[10] I see this as one of the most blatant ties to the practices of God's covenant people in a book where blatant ties are almost non-existent. That this detail is mentioned three times is significant. It gives us a glimpse of God's people acting like God's people even in at the far edges of exile.

Incidentally, God's people didn't always act like it, even when they *were* in the place God had given them—we can be in the right place with the wrong heart. In the book of Joshua, after the Israelites conquered Jericho, they suffered a terrible defeat at the hands of a lesser army at Ai. Joshua was distraught over why this had happened and pleaded with the Lord for an answer.

READ JOSHUA 7:11-12,20-26.

What was Achan guilty of (vv. 20-21)?

Israel's corporate guilt is described in verses 11-12. They took what was:

Valuable	Hidden	Sacred	Set Apart/Consecrated

This account is a sobering reminder that not only does our sin affect others but it is far more serious in the eyes of the Lord than we often think. God had set the plunder apart for destruction (Josh. 7:1) so that Israel would not fall into idolatry and out of love with God. Achan's sin was not only about disobedience but also about covetousness. It was about profiting from another's loss. It was about a lack of trust in God's provisions for him.

Personal Take: The Jews in Esther's day did not take the spoils of those who attacked them even though the letter of the law allowed for it. In what ways does this show their faith in God? Try to be specific.

In response to this question, a friend said she believed that one of the reasons the Jews didn't take the plunder was because they were so overjoyed at their deliverance, they had no need for more. She likened this to our salvation in Christ. "So often we're discontented even though we've been rescued by Christ and given so many blessings. We want more and more," she said. "But when we're overcome by the blessing of our salvation, we don't need anything else. We don't have to go after the plunder." I loved this insight.

READ PHILIPPIANS 4:11-13.

GOSPEL MOMENT

In what area of your life are you currently discontent? Ask the Lord to be your strength in this situation and to give you a contented heart.

Nowhere in the empire of Persia did the Jews put their hands on the plunder. This is reason for celebration! The exiled Jews understood that theirs was a battle of self-defense, a holy war, and not a fight for selfish gain. They were God's people and they were to look and live differently than the multitude of nations around them. It seems that they had a faith that believed God would provide for them even as outsiders in the empire. And perhaps most importantly, they didn't plunder their enemies because they knew having God was infinitely more precious.

Purim

ESTHER 9:20-28

One of the main reasons the book of Esther was written was to tell the story of how the holiday of Purim came to be. The feast of Purim is a special celebration that Jewish people still observe to this day. It is the only feast in the Old Testament that was not commanded by God through Moses. (Hanukkah is also a non-Mosaic feast but the events that inspired it happened after the Old Testament was written.) Purim is characterized by feasting, gift-giving, and full-on celebrating. While some Jewish holidays can be solemn, Purim is not one of them—if ever there was a time to don your party hat during Bible study, today is the day.

READ ESTHER 9:20-28.

Why did the holiday come to be known as Purim (vv. 24-26)?

What was the purpose of Purim (v. 28)?

Holidays and traditions help shape the rhythms of our lives. They bring meaning and memories to different parts of our year. They thread us to our past and inspire us to leave similar threads of special foods, customs, and faith to future generations. Our Christian holidays are often days of rest, feasting, and thanksgiving. Mostly, they help us remember.

Personal Take: What is one of your favorite customs or traditions tied to a Christian holiday? How does that tradition help you remember and reflect on what God has done for you and why?

Mordecai sent his letter about this newly instituted holiday to the Jews both _____ and _____ (v. 20). (Refer back to the map on p. 22 to recall the magnitude of this area.)

The imagery of Jewish celebration "both near and far" is inspiring. Purim would be for the Jew in Susa selling her wares, freshly reminded that she is still one of God's own all the way in a pagan empire. Purim would be for the old man who followed Zerubbabel back to Jerusalem with a hammer in his hand to work on the Temple. Celebrations of deliverance were to dot the landscape spanning a potential 2,000 miles![11]

READ ISAIAH 57:14-21. What word does the Lord speak to those far and near?

Victory   Blessing   Strength   Peace

It's possible that Mordecai understood this great deliverance as a fulfillment of Isaiah's prophecy. In response, the Jews would celebrate on the 14th and 15th of Adar. (Mordecai was probably not advocating for a two-day celebration, rather for the rural Jews to celebrate on the 14th and those within the city walls on the 15th.) Perhaps you're wondering why Mordecai didn't institute the holiday on the actual day of battle (13th), something similar to our Fourth of July.

LOOK BACK AT ESTHER 9:21-22. What reason is given at the top of verse 22?

Your translation may say that the Jews gained "rest" or "relief" from their enemies. The Hebrew is rich with meaning: "to rest, to settle, to settle down . . . freedom, respite from one's enemies."[12]

Personal Take: How might the celebration of God-given rest or relief look different than the celebration of victory in battle?

By the Jews celebrating their deliverance, "the Purim festival is stripped of military overtones and the idea of vengeance on enemies. Instead, it is more closely associated with the positive concepts of enjoying rest and expressing community, joy and gratitude."[13]

I love this insight. I would also add that when we focus on God's gift of freedom and rest, we glory in Him instead of in our strength, achievement, or power to gain victory. The glory goes to Him.

Rest for God's people was woven into the fabric of Creation. On the seventh day, God rested. And He gave that rest to us in the form of the Sabbath. In Christ we have the gift of peace and rest that can be enjoyed every minute of every day. In my younger years, when I was chasing all manner of achievement and pleasure, peace was low on my list. Now, it is one of the things I treasure the most.

READ HEBREWS 4:9-11.

Personal Prayer: What is causing you unrest? Where are you lacking peace? Write a prayer asking the Lord to help you receive His rest in whatever your circumstances.

The remaining part of Esther 9:22 is one of those verses where we want to pitch our tent for a bit. **REREAD ESTHER 9:22.**

Sorrow/Grief was turned into _____

Mourning was turned into _____

Mordecai mentioned four characteristics of the days of Purim. What are they? (I filled in the first one for you.)

1. Feasting

2. _____

3. Sending gifts to _____

4. And to _____

You may remember that at the top of our study we considered the questions the Jews of Esther's day may have been asking themselves. Among them were, *Are we still God's covenant people?* and *Do His promises still apply to us?* The decisive victory over their enemies on the 13th and 14th days of Adar must have felt like a resounding "yes!" In response to God's great deliverance, they would naturally celebrate in keeping with their past customs.

READ DEUTERONOMY 16:16-17. What were the appointed men to bring every year at the time of each festival?

TURN FORWARD TO NEHEMIAH 8:10-12. Who were the Jews to send rich portions of food to?

Personal Take: Why do you think it was important to Mordecai that Purim be a day of gift-giving?

Gift-giving was an important part of Jewish culture and festivals. To be generous to others was to serve as a reminder that God had been generous to Israel. The practice of giving portions of food to one another and to the poor was instituted by God and part of Israel's DNA. That this would take on even greater meaning in the New Testament is not surprising. Jesus's care for the poor and the charge He gave His followers to do the same is a radical example we are to follow as His church. The grace He has given us is to be extended to those both "near and far."

GOSPEL MOMENT

LET'S CLOSE TODAY BY READING ACTS 2:38-39.

What gift was given at Pentecost?

The promise of forgiveness of sin and of the Spirit was for the believers' children and all who were _____.

God has saved us, the ones who were far off. Each of us is invited to celebrate this gift of freedom daily, this "relief" from the enemies of sin, shame, and bondage. Today may not be Purim, or Christmas, or Easter, but it's a day for rejoicing.

Personal Response: In response to the lavish gift of God's Son and His Spirit, what gift can you give someone today? It can be a gift of encouragement, a gift of a meal, a gift of money, the gift of a listening ear, whatever the Spirit brings to your mind. As you give, be reminded of the gift you've been given.

Note from Kelly: *As Purim continues to be celebrated around the world today, one of the things the holiday is most known for are Hamantaschen cookies. These cookies, named for Haman's hat, are a tri-cornered cookie with a fruit filling. You can find many different recipes for these cookies online, and they would make a great treat for your Bible study group!*

Purim
TODAY

Every year, on the eve of Purim (the 13th day of the Hebrew month Adar, or March), Jewish observers fast to commemorate the risk Esther took on behalf of her people. The scroll of Esther is read aloud to close the day. On the 14th of Adar, the morning of Purim, the celebration begins. Esther is read again in its entirety. Children dress up as main characters in the story, and when Haman's name is mentioned, loud *boo*s bellow from the participants, who rattle homemade shakers to drown out his name. The mood is light. Jokes are told and songs are sung. Two types of gifts are given as well: parcels of food for family and friends and charitable gifts to the poor. On the evening of Purim, the Jews gather together for a festive meal.

As I was finishing up this study, my sister forwarded me an email from one her coworkers with the subject, "Hamantaschen (Purim Cookies) in the Kitchen!" Her friend is Jewish and had celebrated Purim the previous weekend. He brought in Hamantaschen (pronounced Hah-men-tah-shen) cookies to share with his colleagues, triangle-shaped pastries that have corners filled with sweet fillings. These cookies are said to mimic Haman's three-cornered hat, symbolizing the sweetness of the Jews' victory. They are a common treat of Purim.

The celebration of Purim continues because God's faithfulness is enduring.

In his email, he gave a brief synopsis of the book of Esther and noted that the spirit of giving is essential to Purim, hence treating his office to cookies. He further explained the fun-loving elements of Purim, one that even includes dressing up in costumes. When I read his email, I was moved by the enduring and far-reaching nature of this holiday, one that Esther and Mordecai instituted more than twenty-five hundred years prior in an empire an ocean away from my sister's workplace. Here, in our modern day, all around the globe, the celebration of Purim continues because God's faithfulness is enduring. "The book of Esther is part of our heritage as Christians. It's part of the big story of redemption that shows God's love for humanity by bringing someone from the line of Abraham to save humankind."[14] Since Christ came through the Jews for the Jews and to be a blessing to all nations, we as God's people today can join in the appreciation and celebration of what God did for His people in Esther.

Singing Songs *in* *a* Foreign Land

ESTHER 9:29-32

The ending of something is always more meaningful when we consider its beginning. As the book of Esther closes with Mordecai second in command of the empire, Esther on the queen's throne, and the resounding deliverance of the Jews, we can't forget that this story blossomed out of the soil of Israel's most devastating season—exile. A little over a century before the first Purim, the freshly deported Jews in Babylon wondered how they would ever survive—much less flourish—outside of Jerusalem. One psalm in particular expresses their grief with provocative imagery.

READ PSALM 137:1-6. (Note: Zion refers to Jerusalem.) Why did the exiles weep by the rivers of Babylon?

Jerusalem was where the Jews flocked to the temple to worship the one, true God. Jerusalem was the city in which the priests mediated on behalf of the people. Jerusalem was where God's presence dwelt. The exiles were terrified of forgetting it. Perhaps they thought if they forgot the city they would forget their God.

Write down the question posed in Psalm 137:4.

Personal Reflection: It's hard to imagine the despair the exiles felt as they sat on the foreign banks of Babylon. Yet you can probably remember a time when your grief or loneliness was so great you wondered if you'd ever be able to sing joyful songs to the Lord again. Write briefly about that season and how the Lord brought you hope. If you're in the middle of that difficult time right now, write about your identification with God's people in Psalm 137.

In 539 BC, approximately fifty years before Ahasuerus's reign, many Jews returned to Jerusalem under King Cyrus. Perhaps one of the first things they looked forward to doing was plucking their harps, loosening their tongues, and singing the praises of their youth in their homeland. *But most exiles did not return.* They and their sons and daughters, grandsons and granddaughters, had made a life outside of Judah. Many may have forgotten the glory of Jerusalem and how to sing the Lord's songs. Maybe a few of them rehearsed the melodies in their heads and hearts, realizing that the Lord inhabited their praises even in the pagan fortress of Persia.

What we do know is that the triumphs of the Jews across the empire were inconceivable to anyone other than God Himself. Only He could have placed Esther and Mordecai in royal positions, giving a future and a hope to those who had hung up their harps on Babylonian poplar trees so many years before.

READ ESTHER 9:29-32.

It may seem redundant for a second letter to go out to the empire confirming the first. But confirmation and reconfirmation are an important part of chapter 9.[15] (I have a tendency to over-communicate, so I personally appreciate the reconfirmation of a confirmation of that which has already been confirmed.) The extra authorization is most certainly due to the magnitude of establishing a new Jewish holiday, something that hadn't happened since the days of Moses.

In addition to Mordecai, who authored this second letter instituting Purim (and was part of the first according to verse 31)?

Circle below. Esther is said to have written with (v. 29) . . .

| Partial authority | Full authority | Mordecai's authority | Ahasuerus's authority |

Karen Jobes writes, "No other woman among God's people wrote with authority to confirm and establish a religious practice that still stands today. The importance of most biblical women, such as Sarah and Hannah, lies in their motherhood. Esther's importance to the covenant people is not as a mother, but as a queen."[16]

Personal Reflection: God gave significant authority to Esther, a woman, in a patriarchal society. How does this encourage or challenge you as you think of the ways you can serve God in your current setting?

We can learn a great deal from the remarkable partnership between Esther and Mordecai and how it reflects God's design. He created male and female to work together to accomplish His kingdom purposes (Gen 1:26-28). While pride, power, and pettiness continually try to undermine His created order, how much more can we in Christ model this beautiful partnership for the world.

Personal Reflection: What aspect of Mordecai and Esther's male/female partnership inspires and/or challenges you as you reflect on how God used them together?

Whether you're a mother, businesswoman, missionary, caretaker, full-time student—or queen—you are to steward your God-given authority and resources for His kingdom purposes. Neither Esther nor Mordecai could have saved the Jews alone. God ordained their partnership to bring about a great deliverance.

> What two words characterized Mordecai's letters, according to verse 30?

> What two practices are mentioned in verse 31?

Esther 9:30-31 seems to have ties to Zechariah 8:19. There the prophet wrote, "The fasts of the fourth, fifth, seventh and tenth months will become joyful and glad occasions and happy festivals for Judah. Therefore love truth and peace." In other words, feasting would replace fasting. Purim would signify the final reversal of all the weeping and wailing the days of fasting represented.[17]

Whether or not Esther and Mordecai wrote their letters with Zechariah in mind, their point appears to be this: As dedicated as we were to fasting and crying out in our times of trouble, so we must be just as committed to celebrating when God delivers![18] Does anyone else need to hear that besides me? Sometimes we don't mourn over tragedy, brokenness, or sin enough. But other times we don't commit to celebrating the redemption God has brought about in our lives.

Personal Response: What is something God has done in your life that is worth celebrating? Make a plan to mark its significance. It could be as big as planning a dinner party, or simply treating yourself to a latte and a few minutes of quiet reflection and prayer. You don't have to institute a national holiday to commemorate what God has done in your life.

Purim celebrates the divine reversal God brought about for Esther and her people. And it points forward to an even further-reaching reversal that would extend beyond the borders of the Persian empire, one that would span the entire globe. Jesus's death on the cross didn't merely improve our circumstances or make us a little less sinful. His death completely reversed the trajectory of our lives.

GOSPEL MOMENT

READ THE FOLLOWING VERSES AND <u>UNDERLINE</u> THE SPECIFIC REVERSALS THAT ARE MENTIONED.

Truly I tell you, anyone who hears my word and believes him who sent me has eternal life and will not come under judgment but has passed from death to life.

JOHN 5:24

He made the one who did not know sin to be sin for us, so that in him we might become the righteousness of God.

2 CORINTHIANS 5:21

What does the reversal of death to life and sin to righteousness mean to you personally?

Christ took upon Himself the judgment that was due us and gave us His righteousness instead. No greater reversal has there ever been or ever will be.

A Rising Star

ESTHER 10:1-3

The book of Esther ends somewhat abruptly by our modern standards. Fortunately, the end of Esther is not really the end. Because of God's great deliverance, the Jewish people continued to thrive, though not without opposition. A little less than five hundred years after Esther's and Mordecai's governance, God set another deliverance in motion. A baby was born in Bethlehem to a young virgin named Mary and to her husband Joseph, whose lineage could be traced to King David. This time, salvation would come not only to the Jews but to all people. But before we arrive in Bethlehem, we'll savor the end of Esther together.

FINISH READING THE FINAL THREE VERSES OF ESTHER, (10:1-3). What did the king impose on his empire?

It's evident the king needed money for his empire. This makes sense when we look back at what Haman had promised to do for the king when he set out his decree to kill the Jewish people.

LOOK BACK AT ESTHER 3:9. What was Haman willing to pay the king to destroy the Jews?

According to 3:13, what did Haman propose the enemy of the Jews could do on the 13th of Adar?

Plunder the Jews   Tax the Jews   Steal from the Jews' harvest

If you were hoping that Esther would end with the king announcing a big tax hike, I am here to make that wish come true. At first blush this detail seems out of place. But it's possible that Mordecai's leadership is steering the king away from bribes and plundering, and toward peaceful taxation.[19] In other words, Mordecai may have understood that wisdom and honesty would grow the empire's coffers, not manipulation and violence. The detail about taxation may also signal that after extraordinary tumult the palace is back to normal life. And nothing says "back to normal" like paying your taxes.

In what annals (or book) were Mordecai's rank and accomplishments recorded (v. 2)?

Centuries before Mordecai rose to fame in a foreign empire, a Hebrew man named Joseph similarly ascended to power in the foreign land of Egypt. God blessed His people under Joseph's leadership, and they enjoyed favor under Pharaoh. But something tragic happened years later.

READ EXODUS 1:6-11.

Who did the new Egyptian king not know about (v. 8)?

What happened to God's people as a result?

Personal Take: Given what happened in Exodus 1, why is it important that Mordecai's story be preserved for future generations?

The final three verses of Esther are meaningful, but you have to dig for some of that meaning! The preservation of Mordecai's story in the "Book of Historical Events" may have helped protect the future generations of the Jews in Persia, as well as the holiday of Purim. Since the Jews couldn't point to the Torah (the first five books of the Bible) as support for Purim, this record was especially important.

The final verse of Esther is a beautiful tribute to Mordecai that we can all aspire to. Mordecai acted, and he spoke. According to verse 3,

What did Mordecai do?

What did Mordecai speak?

Verse 3 offers a stark distinction between Haman and Mordecai. Haman had been promoted at one point, but Mordecai became second in command. Haman was known as the enemy of the Jews, while Mordecai was esteemed by the Jews. Haman's life was characterized by greed and selfishness, whereas Mordecai was known by what he did for others.

It's been said, "An inheritance is something you leave for someone. A legacy is something you leave in someone."[20] Mordecai and Esther's selflessness on behalf of God's people achieved a legacy that is still being celebrated today.

Personal Reflection: How does their example encourage you to live sacrificially for the welfare of others? How does it encourage you to speak up when truth and justice are on the line?

The book of Esther ends with Mordecai as second in command of Persia and Esther reigning on the queen's throne. Who could have imagined the exiled Jews would have reached such heights outside the promised land? Only God. And yet, this wasn't the culmination of His story. Over the next four centuries, Persia would fall to Greece, and Greece would fall to Rome. And in approximately 4 BC, in a nondescript town, hundreds of miles from the epicenter of power, a King unlike any other would be born—Jesus. He would sit on the throne of David, and His rule would be everlasting.

Jesus's kingship would look markedly different from all who came before Him. He would not wield a scepter, or wage war on flesh and blood, or throw lavish parties for His own amusement, or oppress the weak. His kingdom would not resemble Persia, Greece, Rome, or any modern Western superpower because He didn't come to bring an empire, He came to bring the kingdom of heaven.

READ MATTHEW 2:1-12.

What physical posture did the wise men take when they saw the Christ Child (v. 11)?

What kingly gifts did they give Him (v. 11)?

From what direction did the wise men come to worship the new King, Jesus (v. 1)?

We don't know for sure where the magi came from, but one of the most plausible options is Persia. Perhaps these pagan astrologers had Jewish neighbors who told them that a star would one day rise out of Israel (Num. 24:17). We can't be sure, but the imagery of Persian stargazers traveling hundreds of miles to seek the King of the Jews drives the book of Esther home in epic fashion.[21]

We began our study with an exiled people, only a few generations removed from the first exiles who had been flung far from their homes. Eventually, many returned to Jerusalem. But most could not. Whether in Babylon, Persia, or somewhere in between, they likely wondered, *Are we still God's?* Then terror came in the form of Haman's decree. In eleven months, every living Jew would be slaughtered. *It seems He has forgotten us*, they feared.

What they didn't know is that a young and orphaned Jewish woman in the king's harem was making her way up the Persian ranks. What they didn't know is that an upstanding man named Mordecai with ties to Israel's monarchy was in the thick of Persia's royal business. What they didn't know, or may have forgotten, is that the God of Judah was also the God of Persia, the God of the whole earth, and the God who created the cosmos. He would go with His people even when His people failed to go with Him.

The empire wasn't beyond His reach, because nothing is.

The news of Israel's God continued to spread until one day an unusual heavenly body caught the eye of pagan stargazers. They'd evidently heard about this rising star from their Jewish neighbors. They would drop everything and follow the star to a King. And when they got there, they would worship. Talk about reversal. Hundreds of years prior, the Jews had traveled west from Jerusalem. Now, it was those from the east leaving their homes for Bethlehem. And eventually, in both directions, Christ's gospel would spread.

Personal Reflection: What has been the most meaningful takeaway from studying the book of Esther?

Craig Blomberg says, "The people least expected to worship the Christ Child come to do so, while those who should have been awaiting him are threatened by his arrival."[22] How often God draws the *least expected*. It was the least expected orphaned exile who became queen of Persia. The least expected Jewish servant in the courts who rose to second in command. The least expected foreign magi who came to worship Jesus.

If we have gained anything from this study, may it be that no one is outside God's reach. That the least expected are often the most invited. And that no matter how far we feel from home, in Christ, we are still the people of God.

Lentil Curry Soup

I simply cannot write a Bible study that doesn't include a soup recipe. I am of the belief that soup can be eaten year-round, never mind how hot it gets in summer. Lentils are also a superfood so you can feel great about this recipe without sacrificing taste—the coconut milk with curry and lime juice make it especially flavorful. Plus, you can find lentils in the Bible.

INGREDIENTS

- 2 tbs coconut oil
- 1 medium onion, chopped
- 4 garlic cloves, minced
- 3 tbs minced fresh ginger
- 1 tbs mild curry powder
- ¼ tsp crushed red pepper flakes, plus more to taste
- 1 (28-ounce) can fire-roasted diced tomatoes

- 1 cup dry French green lentils, rinsed
- 2½-3 cups water (for desired consistency)
- 1 (14-ounce) can full-fat coconut milk
- 1 tsp sea salt plus more to taste
- Ground pepper to taste
- ½ cup chopped fresh cilantro
- 2 tbs fresh lime juice

DIRECTIONS

1. Heat coconut oil in large pot or Dutch oven over medium heat. Add onion and a pinch of salt. Cook until soft, 8 to 10 minutes.

2. Add garlic, ginger, curry powder, and red pepper flakes and cook (turning low if needed), coating onion thoroughly about 2 minutes.

3. Add tomatoes, lentils, water, coconut milk, ½ teaspoon salt, and freshly ground black pepper. Bring to a boil, cover, and reduce heat. Simmer until the lentils are tender, 25 to 35 minutes. Stir occasionally. Add extra ½ cup of water if needed if soup is too thick. Finally, stir in lime juice and top individual bowls with cilantro. I serve with a loaf of sourdough bread and butter.[23]

Watch the Session Seven Video

Use the space below to follow along with the outline points from Kelly's teaching. A leader guide is available for free download at **lifeway.com/estherstudy**.

1. In Jesus Christ there is _____

_____.

To access the video sessions, use the instructions in the back of your Bible study book.

ENDNOTES

Session Two

1. The Editors of Encyclopaedia Britannica, "Babylonia," Encyclopedia Britannica, March 26, 2024, https://www.britannica.com/place/Babylonia.

2. Dates are approximate. Based on the timeline in the *CSB Study Bible*, and supplemented with *Rose Book of Bible Charts, Maps and Timelines* (United States: Rose Publishing, 2015), 120.

3. Mervin Breneman, *Ezra, Nehemiah, Esther*, electronic ed., vol. 10, The New American Commentary (Nashville: Broadman & Holman Publishers, 1993), 304.

4. Russell L. Meek, "Nehemiah in Susa," *Nehemiah, a Commentary*, accessed May 10, 2024, https://www.thegospelcoalition.org/commentary/nehemiah/#section-7

5. Eds. Encyclopaedia Britannica, "Israel," Encyclopedia Britannica, June 8, 2024, https://www.britannica.com/topic/Israel-Old-Testament-kingdom.

6. Eds. Encyclopaedia Britannica, "Judah," Encyclopedia Britannica, November 14, 2023, https://www.britannica.com/topic/Judah-Hebrew-tribe.

7. Iain M. Duguid, *Esther and Ruth*, eds. R. D. Phillips & P. G. Ryken, Reformed Expository Commentary (Phillipsburg, NJ: P&R Publishing 2005) 4.

8. Joyce G. Baldwin, *Esther: An Introduction and Commentary*, vol. 12, Tyndale Old Testament Commentaries (Downers Grove, IL: InterVarsity Press, 1984), 57.

9. Breneman, 305.

10. Karen H. Jobes, *Esther*, The NIV Application Commentary (Grand Rapids, MI: Zondervan, 1999), 62.

11. Jobes, 67.

12. Jon D. Levenson, *Esther: A Commentary* (United States: Presbyterian Publishing Corporation, 1997), 12.

13. Brenemen 307-308.

14. Jobes, 73.

15. Duguid, 15.

16. Jen Wooster, "Lamb Vindaloo," Peel with Zeal, December 29, 2022, https://www.peelwithzeal.com/lamb-vindaloo-recipe/.

Session Three

1. Adele Berlin, *Esther: The Traditional Hebrew Text with the New JPS Translation* (United States: Jewish Publication Society, 2001), 23.

2. Michael V. Fox, *Character and Ideology in the Book of Esther* (United States: W.B. Eerdmans, 2001) 34.

3. Ibid.

4. Richard S. Hess, *Israelite Religions: An Archaeological and Biblical Survey*, electronic ed. (Grand Rapids: Baker Academic, 2007), 193.

5. Baldwin, 66.

6. Eds. Encyclopaedia Britannica, "Diaspora," Encyclopedia Britannica, May 29, 2024, https://www.britannica.com/topic/Diaspora-Judaism.

7. Baldwin, 65.

8. Robert R. Cargill, "Hello My Name Is: Esther," Bible and Archaeology (University of Iowa), August 11, 2023, https://bam.sites.uiowa.edu/hello/esther.

9. Levenson, 58.

10. Baldwin, 66.

11. Jobes, 98.

12. "Strong's H2617," Blue Letter Bible, accessed June 17, 2024, https://www.blueletterbible.org/lexicon/h2617/esv/wlc/0-1/.

13. Baldwin, 68.

14. Ibid, 68-69.

15. Breneman, 313–314.

16. Debra Reid, *Esther: An Introduction and Commentary*, vol. 13, Tyndale Old Testament Commentaries (Downers Grove, IL: InterVarsity Press, 2008), 74.

17. Jobes, 109-114.

18. Warren Baker and Eugene E. Carpenter, *The Complete Word Study Dictionary: Old Testament* (Chattanooga, TN: AMG Publishers, 2003), 176.

19. K. L. Barker, J. H. Stek, M. L. Strauss, & R. F. Youngblood, *Zondervan NIV study Bible: Notes and Introductions* (Grand Rapids, MI: Zondervan, 2008), 2107.

20. Timothy George, "Providence," *Holman Bible Dictionary*, ed. Trent C. Butler, accessed May 20, 2024, https://www.studylight.org/dictionaries/eng/hbd/p/providence.html.

21. Walter A. Elwell, "Providence of God," BibleStudyTools.com, accessed May 20, 2024, https://www.biblestudytools.com/dictionary/providence-of-god/.

22. Fox, 44-45.

23. Duguid.

24. Reid, 92.

25. Thanks to Dr. Craig Blomberg for his many insights into Esther.

26. Duguid, 36.

27. Reid, 93.

28. Corrie ten Boom, John Sherill, Elizabeth Sherill, *The Hiding Place* (Baker Publishing Group: 2015).

Session Four

1. Oxford English Dictionary, "lament (v.)," September 2023, https://doi.org/10.1093/OED/3450353976.

2. Breneman, 334.

3. Mark Vroegop, *Dark Clouds, Deep Mercy* (United States: Crossway, 2019), 28.

4. Colleen Houde, "TN Pastor Returns to Pulpit Months After Daughter Killed in Mass Shooting," The Roys Report, May 31, 2023, https://julieroys.com/tn-pastor-returns-to-pulpit-months-after-daughter-killed-mass-shooting/.

5. Levenson, 80.

6. Duguid, 49.

7. Duguid.

8. I thank Dr. Craig Blomberg for his insight into Romans 8:28.

9. Fox, 205.

10. Baldwin, 82.

11. Duguid, 52.

12. Kelly Minter, *Encountering God: Cultivating Habits of Faith Through Spiritual Disciplines* (Nashville: Lifeway Press, 2023), 97.

13. Fox, 205.

14. Fox, 67.

15. Jobes, 146.

16. Leland Ryken, as quoted by Jobes, 138.

17. Recipe inspired by a recipe from Half Baked Harvest.

Session Five

1. Matthew Perry, *Friends, Lovers, and the Big Terrible Thing: A Memoir* (New York: Flatiron Books, 2022).

2. Jobes, 153.

3. Ibid.

4. Commonly attributed to Charles H. Spurgeon, as quoted by David Platt, "Sovereignty of God (1 Samuel 19:10)," Radical Podcast, August 27, 2021, https://radical.net/podcasts/pray-the-word/sovereignty-of-god-1-samuel-1910/.

5. Tremper Longman III, *Psalms: An Introduction and Commentary*, ed. David G. Firth, vol. 15–16, Tyndale Old Testament Commentaries (Nottingham, England: InterVarsity Press, 2014), 278.

6. Breneman, 346.

Session Six

1. Jobes, 158.

2. Fox, 86.

3. Ibid.

4. Jobes, 165.

5. Fox, 88

6. Ibid.

7. Fox, 87. Levenson 104-105.

8. Fox, 243.

9. Peter Leithart, "Hamas is Borrowing Tactics from the Amalekites," The Gospel Coalition, October 13, 2023, https://www.thegospelcoalition.org/article/hamas-tactics-amalekites/.

10. Jobes, 168.

11. Leithart.

12. Jobes, 189.

13. Baldwin, 96.

14. John Stott, *The Message of the Sermon on the Mount* (United Kingdom: InterVarsity Press, 2020).

15. Jobes, 40–41.

16. Baldwin, 98.

17. Justin Jackson, "Raised up from the Dust: An Exploration of Hannah's Reversal Motif in the Book of Esther as Evidence of Divine Sovereignty," *Themelios*, Vol. 46 Issue 3, https://www.thegospelcoalition.org/themelios/article/raised-up-from-the-dust/.

Session Seven

1. Breneman, 363.

2. Fox, 108.

3. Ibid., 109.

4. Ibid., 108.

5. Jobes ,183-193.

6. Ibid., 184.

7. Fox, 112.

8. Duguid, 115. Reid, 142. Fox, 112. Levenson, 122.

9. Lewis Bayles Paton, *A Critical and Exegetical Commentary on the Book of Esther* (New York, Charles Scribner's Sons, 1908), 287.

10. Jobes, 196.

11. Baldwin, 108.

12. Warren Baker and Eugene E. Carpenter, *The Complete Word Study Dictionary: Old Testament* (Chattanooga, TN: AMG Publishers, 2003), 716.

13. Reid, 146–147.

14. Dominick Hernández, "Feast of Purim: God's Silent and Surprising Deliverance," The Gospel Coalition, March 6, 2023, https://www.thegospelcoalition.org/article/silent-surprising-purim/.

15. Fox, 124.

16. Jobes 224.

17. Reid, 149.

18. Ibid.

19. Levenson, 132.

20. Reggie Joiner, *Think Orange: Imagine the Impact When Church and Family Collide* (Colorado Springs: David C. Cook, 2009).

21. Craig Blomberg, *Matthew*, vol. 22, The New American Commentary (Nashville: Broadman & Holman Publishers, 1992), 62.

22. Craig Blomberg, *Jesus and the Gospels: An Introduction and Survey* (United States: B&H Publishing Group, 2009), 200.

23. Recipe inspired by www.loveandlemons.com

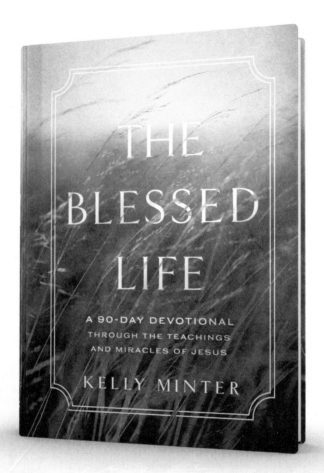

ADDITIONAL STUDIES FROM KELLY MINTER

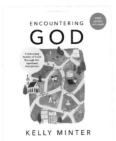

ENCOUNTERING GOD
Cultivating Habits of Faith Through the Spiritual Disciplines
7 sessions

Unpack the biblical foundation for spiritual disciplines, including ways to practice disciplines like prayer, study, worship, rest, simplicity, generosity, celebration, and more.

lifeway.com/encounteringgod

WHAT LOVE IS
The Letters of 1, 2, 3 John
7 sessions

Delve into the letters of 1, 2, and 3 John, written to encourage followers of Jesus to remain faithful to the truth. Glimpse not only the heart of John but also the heart of Jesus.

lifeway.com/whatloveis

FINDING GOD FAITHFUL
A Study on the Life of Joseph
8 sessions

Trace the path of Joseph's life in the book of Genesis to observe how God's sovereignty reigns, even in our darkest moments.

lifeway.com/findinggodfaithful

NEHEMIAH
A Heart That Can Break
7 sessions

Nehemiah's heart was so broken for those in need that he left the comfort of his Persian palace to help them. Are you ready to let God break your heart for a hurting, lost world and move you to be the hands and feet of Jesus?

lifeway.com/nehemiah

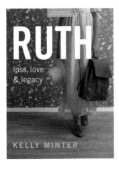

RUTH
Loss, Love & Legacy
7 sessions

Walk through the book of Ruth and discover God's faithfulness in suffering, His immeasurable grace where we least expect it, and the way Ruth's story points toward Jesus.

lifeway.com/ruth

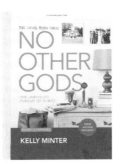

NO OTHER GODS
The Unrivaled Pursuit of Christ
8 sessions

Learn to identify the functional gods you may unknowingly be serving to experience the abundant life only Jesus can give.

lifeway.com/noothergods

ALL THINGS NEW
A Study on 2 Corinthians
8 sessions

Study the letter of 2 Corinthians to discover how God can use you no matter your situation.

lifeway.com/allthingsnew

lifeway.com/kellyminter
800.458.2772

Lifeway women

Pricing and availability subject to change without notice.

Get the most from your study.

Customize your Bible study time with a guided experience.

In this study you'll:

- Discover how Esther's story inspires us to live faithfully and courageously in our own time
- Understand how the book of Esther fits into God's redemptive story
- Be reminded that God is always at work in every place and at all times
- See how God uses faithful men and women working together to accomplish His redemptive purposes in the world

STUDYING ON YOUR OWN?

Watch Kelly Minter's teaching sessions, available via redemption code for individual video-streaming access, printed in this Bible study book.

LEADING A GROUP?

Each group member will need an Esther Bible study book, which includes video access. Because all participants will have access to the video content, you can choose to watch the videos outside of your group meeting if desired. Or, if you're watching together and someone misses a group meeting, they'll have the flexibility to catch up! A DVD set is also available to purchase separately if desired.

Browse study formats, a free session sample, leader guide, video clips, church promotional materials, and more at

lifeway.com/estherstudy

HERE'S YOUR VIDEO ACCESS.

To stream *Esther* Bible study video teaching sessions, follow these steps:

1. Go to my.lifeway.com/redeem and register or log in to your Lifeway account.

2. Enter this redemption code to gain access to your individual-use video license:

NGSSB5BW42DJ

Once you've entered your personal redemption code, you can stream the video teaching sessions any time from your Digital Media page on my.lifeway.com or watch them via the Lifeway On Demand app on any TV or mobile device via your Lifeway account.

There's no need to enter your code more than once! To watch your streaming videos, just log in to your Lifeway account at my.lifeway.com or watch using the Lifeway On Demand app.

QUESTIONS? WE HAVE ANSWERS!
Visit support.lifeway.com and search "Video Redemption Code" or call our Tech Support Team at 866.627.8553.